Access

GCSE ENGLISH LITERATURE

for OCR

Alison Smith

D. C. Coleman
Chief Examiner

Annie Fox
Garrett O'Doherty
Angela Topping
Carmel Waldron

OCR
RECOGNISING ACHIEVEMENT
OXFORD
UNIVERSITY PRESS
Official Publisher Partnership

Contents

How to Use This Book

Welcome to your GCSE English Literature course!

The aim of this book is to prepare you for the OCR GCSE English Literature exams and Controlled Assessments. In the following chapters you will find plenty of fun and interesting activities to build your skills and knowledge, and also all the help and advice you need for your assessments.

This book includes a range of **useful features**.

- **How to approach** sections explain what you need to do for each part of the specification.

- **Preparing for** sections offer helpful guidance on preparing for exams and Controlled Assessments to help you achieve your best results.

- **Learning checklists** at the start of each chapter explain the Assessment Objectives and tell you what skills will be covered in the pages that follow.

- **Annotated source texts** provide useful notes to help you understand key words and identify key points.

The book is made up of four units:
- **Unit 1:** Literary Heritage Linked Texts
- **Unit 2:** Modern Drama
- **Unit 3:** Prose from Different Cultures
- **Unit 4:** Literary Heritage Prose and Contemporary Poetry.

Each of these units is assessed using **Assessment Objectives**. The four Assessment Objectives (AOs) for English Literature are:

AO1

- Respond to texts critically and imaginatively.
- Select and evaluate relevant textual detail to illustrate and support interpretations.

AO2

- Explain how language, structure and form contribute to writers' presentation of ideas, themes and settings.

AO3

- Make comparisons and explain links between texts.
- Evaluate writers' different ways of expressing meaning and achieving effects.

AO4

- Link texts to their social, cultural and historical contexts.
- Explain the influence of texts on yourself and different readers in different places and times.

Unit 1
Literary Heritage Linked Texts

HOW TO APPROACH UNIT 1

What will be assessed in this unit?

Unit 1 is split into two parts:

- Shakespeare and Film/Audio/Live Performance
- Literary Heritage Poetry.

The whole unit is worth 25% of the English Literature GCSE.

How will this unit be assessed?

Unit 1 is tested through Controlled Assessment. You will write **two** extended essays, one about a Shakespeare play and the other about two poems by the same poet.

You will have plenty of time to think about the tasks, discuss them in class and get to know the texts before you write anything.

What are controlled conditions?

When you write your final response to each task, you will not be able to talk to other students or get help from your teacher. You will need more than one writing session to complete your work, so you must hand in what you have written at the end of each session. It will be given back to you at the start of the next session.

Can I take notes into the assessment?

You can take one sheet of **A4 notes** into your assessment.

What play will I study?

You will study the written form of **one** of the following plays together with a film version, an audio version or a live performance of the same play:

- *Julius Caesar*
- *Macbeth*
- *The Merchant of Venice*
- *Romeo and Juliet.*

What will the task be?

There will be **one task** set on your chosen play. You will have to comment on part of the written form of the play as well as the other version.

How will the task be marked?

This task will be marked on Assessment Objectives 1 and 3.

- **AO1:** You need to show how you interpret the text, using close reference to the text to explain your ideas.
- **AO3:** You need to identify similarities and differences between the written version of the play and a film or audio version, or a live performance.

The quality of your writing will also be assessed. This means that you need to check that:

- your writing is easy to read
- your use of spelling, punctuation and grammar is correct
- your style of writing is suitable for the task.

Responding to a Shakespeare Text

LEARNING CHECKLIST

In this chapter you will learn to:

1 Respond to the text with insight and imagination.

2 Use quotations to support your ideas.

AO1

Why is Shakespeare still studied and performed?

William Shakespeare (1564–1616) lived and wrote hundreds of years ago, but his plays are still performed and studied around the world. Why?

ACTIVITY 1

a Read the opinions below. Decide whether you agree or disagree with them and why.

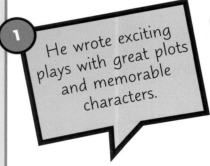

1 He wrote exciting plays with great plots and memorable characters.

2 He's the greatest writer of all time. Everyone should know at least one of his plays.

3 His plays deal with themes that everyone can relate to like love, death, friendship and revenge.

b Write a paragraph explaining why you think Shakespeare is still studied and performed.

What is interpretation?

An **interpretation** is a point of view about the meaning of a text. Different directors might present the same play in different ways by:

- highlighting a key theme, such as war or prejudice
- changing the setting to a certain time period to make it more relevant or dramatic.

Stagecraft: how to analyse a play

Plays are set out differently from other texts because they are written to be performed in front of an audience. The key features of a play are:

Characters
the roles that the actors play.

Dialogue
the words that the characters speak.

Stage directions
instructions telling the actors what to do, or what is to happen.

Shakespeare's plays are usually divided into two main categories: comedies and tragedies. Look at the common features of each, below.

Shakespeare's comedies
- disguise or mistaken identity
- unusual settings
- humorous characters
- happy endings, often with a marriage

Shakespeare's tragedies
- the main character is the tragic hero who has a high status
- the tragic hero has a flaw such as ambition or jealousy
- something bad happens to the tragic hero
- the play ends with death

ACTIVITY 2

a Copy and complete the spider diagram with examples from the play you are studying. Underline **comic** features with a solid line and **tragic** elements with a dotted line.

b Write a paragraph explaining why you think the play is a comedy or a tragedy or a mix of both.

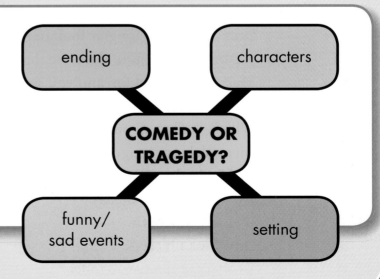

ending

characters

COMEDY OR TRAGEDY?

funny/ sad events

setting

Characterization: Lady Macbeth

Lady Macbeth can be interpreted in many different ways. Some people think she is evil and ambitious. Others think she is fragile and disturbed.

Read the scene below, which takes place after Lady Macbeth has found out that the witches have predicted that Macbeth will become King. Think about some of the decisions the actor playing Lady Macbeth has to make.

From *Macbeth*
by William Shakespeare

Macbeth
My dearest love,
Duncan comes here tonight.

What tone of voice should she use?

Lady Macbeth
And when goes hence?

Macbeth
Tomorrow, as he purposes.

What might her facial expression be?

Lady Macbeth
O never
Shall sun that morrow see.
Your face, my thane, is as a book where men
May read strange matters. To beguile the time,

How does she try to convince Macbeth to act?

Look like the time, bear welcome in your eye,
Your hand, your tongue; look like th'innocent flower,
But be the serpent under't. He that's coming
Must be provided for, and you shall put
This night's great business into my dispatch,
Which shall to all our nights and days to come
Give solely sovereign sway and masterdom.

What does this metaphor suggest to you?

Macbeth
We will speak further—

Does Lady Macbeth interrupt or does Macbeth trail off?

Lady Macbeth
Only look up clear;
To alter favour ever is to fear.
Leave all the rest to me.

Characterization: Shylock

Shylock in *The Merchant of Venice* is one of Shakespeare's most controversial characters. The actor must decide how sympathetic, frightening or amusing he will make him.

In the scene below, Bassanio approaches Shylock for a loan. Bassanio's friend, Antonio, will be guarantor, which means that he will be responsible for paying the loan back if Bassanio doesn't. As you read it, think about the decisions the actor has to make.

From *The Merchant of Venice*
by **William Shakespeare**

Enter Bassanio *with* Shylock

What are they doing at the beginning of the scene?

Shylock

Three thousand ducats, well.

Bassanio

Ay, sir, for three months.

Shylock

Why does Shylock repeat what Bassanio says?

For three months, well.

Bassanio

For the which, as I told you, Antonio shall be bound.

Shylock

How does Shylock react when he hears Antonio's name?

Antonio shall become bound, well.

Bassanio

May you stead me? Will you pleasure me? Shall I know your answer?

Shylock

Three thousand ducats for three months, and Antonio bound.

Bassanio

Your answer to that?

Shylock

Antonio is a good man—

Bassanio

Have you heard any imputation to the contrary?

Shylock

Later in the scene Shylock says he 'hates' Antonio. Does this hatred begin to show now?

Ho no, no, no, no: my meaning in saying he is a good man is to have you understand me that he is sufficient.

ACTIVITY 3

With a partner, try different ways of acting one of these scenes. Think about your tone of voice, facial expressions and body language. Which lines would you emphasize?

Themes: love in Romeo and Juliet

A **theme** is an important topic or idea that is developed in a text. Often texts will have a number of themes. As you study your play, try to look beyond the basic plot and discover the themes that are being explored.

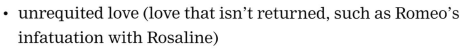

Romeo and Juliet contains themes such as revenge, violence, family and friendship, but the most important theme is **love**. Throughout the play many types of love are explored, such as:

- unrequited love (love that isn't returned, such as Romeo's infatuation with Rosaline)
- love of family (the love of parents for their children)
- romantic love (the deepening love between Romeo and Juliet)
- fatal love (obsessive love that leads to death).

ACTIVITY 4

Read the quotations below from *Romeo and Juliet*. Then copy and complete the grid, noting which type of love you think each quotation shows.

Quotation	Type of love	Explanation
'Love is... a madness most discreet, a choking gall and a preserving sweet.'	Romeo's unrequited (unreturned) love for Rosaline	Romeo is miserable because of his infatuation with Rosaline. He compares it to illness and insanity.
'She's the hopeful lady of my earth.'		
'Thus with a kiss I die.'	fatal love	
'my wife is dead tonight;/ Grief of my son's exile hath stopp'd her breath.'		

Themes: ambition in Macbeth

Macbeth's tragic flaw is his ambition. Although he is successful, he is dissatisfied and does things that he knows are wrong. As he says in Act 1, Scene 7, 'I have no spur/To prick the sides of my intent, but only/Vaulting ambition which o'erleaps itself'.

A director of *Macbeth* would need to decide:
- what makes him ambitious
- which actions are because of his ambition
- what the cost of his ambition is.

ACTIVITY 5

Complete the spider diagram with evidence from *Macbeth* on the theme of ambition. (If you are studying *Julius Caesar*, do the same with that play.)

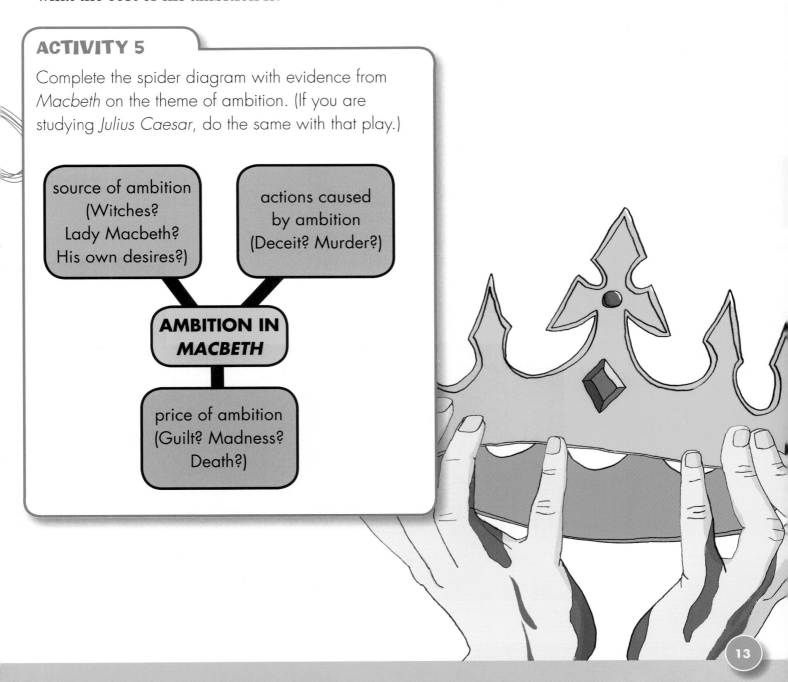

source of ambition
(Witches?
Lady Macbeth?
His own desires?)

actions caused
by ambition
(Deceit? Murder?)

**AMBITION IN
MACBETH**

price of ambition
(Guilt? Madness?
Death?)

Language: revealing characters' emotions

Shakespeare is admired for his use of language. He uses many techniques such as rhyme, metaphor and alliteration. This makes the language sound beautiful and it builds up vivid images for the listener. It also shows us what is happening in the characters' minds.

ACTIVITY 6

Read the extract below. Macbeth has just learned that his wife is dead. What does it show us about his feelings?

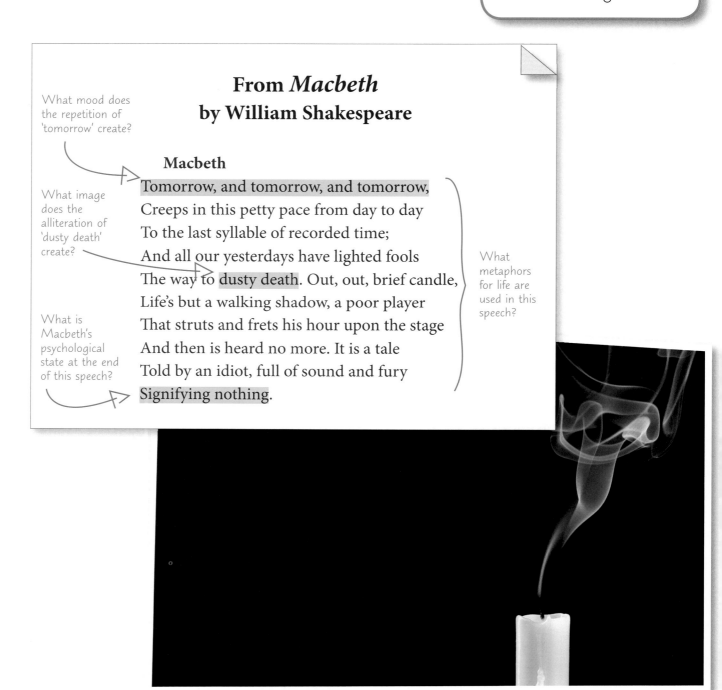

What mood does the repetition of 'tomorrow' create?

What image does the alliteration of 'dusty death' create?

What is Macbeth's psychological state at the end of this speech?

What metaphors for life are used in this speech?

From *Macbeth*
by William Shakespeare

Macbeth

Tomorrow, and tomorrow, and tomorrow,
Creeps in this petty pace from day to day
To the last syllable of recorded time;
And all our yesterdays have lighted fools
The way to dusty death. Out, out, brief candle,
Life's but a walking shadow, a poor player
That struts and frets his hour upon the stage
And then is heard no more. It is a tale
Told by an idiot, full of sound and fury
Signifying nothing.

UNIT 1

Supporting your interpretation of the play

When writing about your play, you must show that you can respond to it by giving your own opinions. You need to support your ideas with quotations from the play. Remember to plan your response carefully before writing it.

ACTIVITY 7

Choose one scene from the Shakespeare play you are studying. Use the grid below to plan your response to that scene.

Aspects to consider	Evidence	Explanation
Comic and/or tragic elements: Is the scene comic or tragic or both?		
Characterization: What do we learn about the characters in this scene? Who is most important?		
Themes: What themes are developed?		
Language: What does the language show about the characters' emotions?		
Importance within the play: How does this scene fit in with the play as a whole? Is it a turning point? Does it give any clues about future events?		
Directorial choices: How should important moments be staged? Think about setting, casting and key ideas.		

LEARNING CHECKLIST

In this chapter, you will learn to:

1 Respond to the text with insight and imagination.

2 Use quotations to support your ideas.

3 Compare and link texts, looking at how different writers express meaning and create effects.

Why film Shakespeare's plays?

Shakespeare's plays have been the inspiration for many films, including musicals (*West Side Story*), modern versions (*10 Things I Hate About You*) and foreign films (*Throne of Blood*). Why? It may be because the strong plots and characters can be updated and adapted to attract a wide audience. Also, special film effects can add to the magic of Shakespeare's language and imagery.

ACTIVITY 1

With a partner, read each point below and discuss whether it is true for theatre, cinema or both:

1 the excitement of seeing a live performance

2 the chance to see famous actors

3 emphasis on the spoken word

4 emphasis on visual images

5 the acting seems very realistic

6 use of close-ups to show what a character is thinking

7 use of soliloquies to show what a character is thinking

8 use of special effects and editing to create excitement.

Using film techniques to convey meaning

When filming a Shakespeare play, the director will have to:

- edit the script so that the film is not too long
- choose whether to use film techniques such as **flashback** to 'show' the audience what has happened rather than 'telling' them
- decide on a setting, for example, in a modern or historic period
- choose actors who can create exciting characters.

ACTIVITY 2

In the grid below are some film techniques that a director might use. Decide how each technique could be used to create a film version of the Shakespeare play you have been studying.

Technique	Definition	Possible uses in a film of a Shakespeare play
voiceover	an unseen voice used to narrate or comment on a film	could be used to introduce the film or used instead of soliloquies
camera shots/ angles	the distance and angle of the camera, which can include close-ups, long shots and high and low angle shots	
editing	how sections of the film are put together, for example: • flashbacks (showing what happened in the past) • montage (a series of short shots) • dissolves (a gradual edit from one scene to another) The frequency of edits and length between cuts may affect the pace of the scene.	
transposition	changing the order of scenes	
soundtrack	the sound accompanying the images, including music and sound effects	

Modernizing Shakespeare: Romeo + Juliet

One of the challenges for a director of a Shakespeare film is how to make it popular. In 1996, director Baz Luhrmann filmed a modern version of *Romeo & Juliet*. Although he used Shakespeare's language, he set the film in a world of TV, helicopters and gunfights, with a rock- and soul-influenced soundtrack. His film was hugely successful.

ACTIVITY 3

The casting of Leonardo Di Caprio and Claire Danes in Baz Luhrmann's film was one key element of its popularity. With a partner, write a casting brief for a new film of the play you are studying. Describe the qualities that the actors playing the leading roles would need.

Think about:
- age
- appearance
- voice
- emotions they would need to show
- previous acting experience.

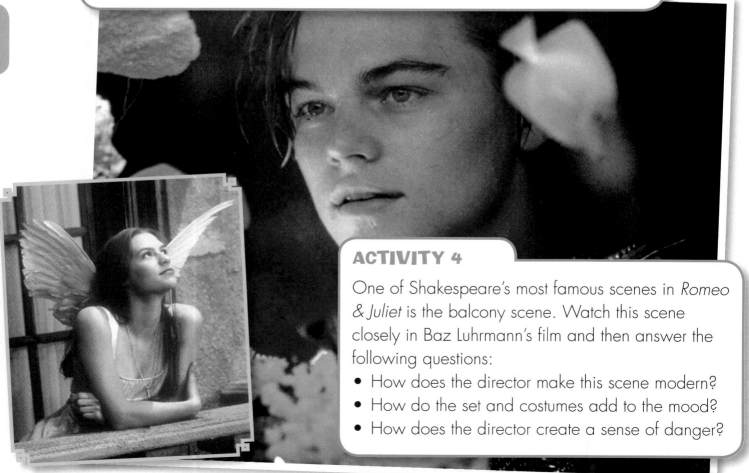

ACTIVITY 4

One of Shakespeare's most famous scenes in *Romeo & Juliet* is the balcony scene. Watch this scene closely in Baz Luhrmann's film and then answer the following questions:
- How does the director make this scene modern?
- How do the set and costumes add to the mood?
- How does the director create a sense of danger?

Acting Shakespeare for film

In 2001, the director Trevor Nunn remade a production of *The Merchant of Venice* for screen. His version is set in 1930s central Europe and stars Henry Goodman as Shylock. In 2004, Al Pacino played Shylock in Michael Radford's film set in Venice in 1596. The films show how different interpretations can be made from one script.

Some techniques that actors use include:

- **vocal skills**: volume, accent, speed and tone of voice
- **facial expressions**: frowns, smiles, raising eyebrows
- **body language**: how they stand and gesture.

ACTIVITY 5

Read Act 1, Scene 3 of *The Merchant of Venice*. Then watch the scene as performed by Henry Goodman and Al Pacino as Shylock in the two different film versions. Copy and complete the grid below with answers to the questions.

Things to think about	2001 film – Henry Goodman	2004 film – Al Pacino
Where is the scene set?		
What is Shylock's reaction to Antonio?		
What stands out about the way Shylock speaks?		
What facial expressions does he use?		
Do you agree with the way he plays Shylock?		

Films and stage productions

Some film versions of Shakespeare's plays are made just for the cinema. Others begin as stage productions which then go on to be filmed.

Trevor Nunn's 1979 film of *Macbeth* uses the plain costumes and simple props and sets from the original theatre production.

In contrast, Roman Polanski's 1971 film uses many cinematic techniques, such as locations, voiceovers and dramatizations of background events.

Before watching Act 2, Scene 2 (Chapter 11 in the Polanski version), read the extract below.

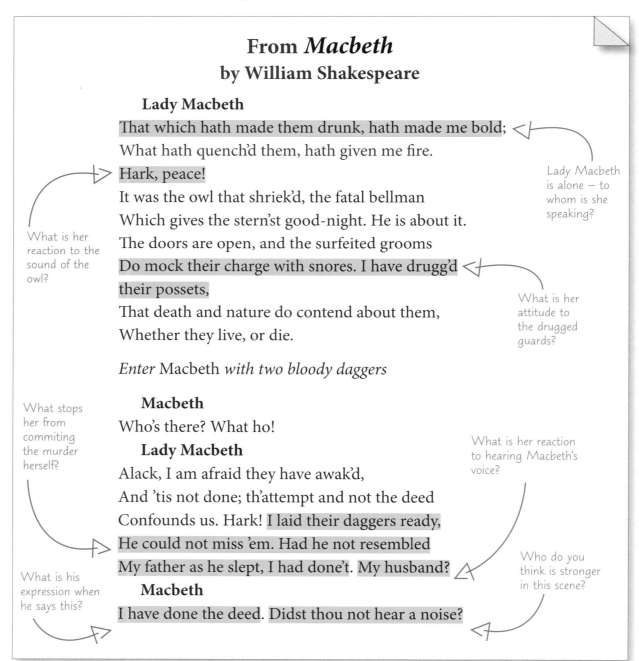

From *Macbeth*
by William Shakespeare

Lady Macbeth

That which hath made them drunk, hath made me bold;

What hath quench'd them, hath given me fire.

Hark, peace!

It was the owl that shriek'd, the fatal bellman

Which gives the stern'st good-night. He is about it.

The doors are open, and the surfeited grooms

Do mock their charge with snores. I have drugg'd their possets,

That death and nature do contend about them,

Whether they live, or die.

Enter Macbeth *with two bloody daggers*

Macbeth

Who's there? What ho!

Lady Macbeth

Alack, I am afraid they have awak'd,

And 'tis not done; th'attempt and not the deed

Confounds us. Hark! I laid their daggers ready,

He could not miss 'em. Had he not resembled

My father as he slept, I had done't. My husband?

Macbeth

I have done the deed. Didst thou not hear a noise?

Annotations:

Lady Macbeth is alone – to whom is she speaking?

What is her reaction to the sound of the owl?

What is her attitude to the drugged guards?

What stops her from commiting the murder herself?

What is his expression when he says this?

What is her reaction to hearing Macbeth's voice?

Who do you think is stronger in this scene?

There are many differences between the two films. For example, Roman Polanski has cut many of the lines and chooses to show Duncan's murder. However, both productions focus on Lady Macbeth thinking about the crime and Macbeth's reaction once 'the deed' has been done.

ACTIVITY 6

Compare how Lady Macbeth is presented in each film. Use the questions in the annotations on Page 20 and a grid like the one below to help you.

	Trevor Nunn's film	Roman Polanski's film
appearance		
Lady Macbeth's emotional state before the murder		
Lady Macbeth's reaction to Macbeth's entrance		
lines given special emphasis		
relationship between Lady Macbeth and Macbeth		
signs of nervousness		
body language		

Identifying with characters

Any interpretation of a play will influence how much we understand and feel sympathy for the characters.

Here is an assessment task on *The Merchant of Venice*.

> Focusing on Act 1, Scene 3; Act 2, Scene 8 and Act 4, Scene 1 of *The Merchant of Venice*, explore to what extent Shylock is portrayed as a victim or a villain.

As a modern audience, we may see things differently from an Elizabethan audience. *The Merchant of Venice* causes much discussion about the behaviour of characters like Portia and Antonio. Some directors suggest that Shylock is a victim of the society in which he lives. Others think he is an evil, twisted character who would not hesitate to take another person's life.

UNIT 1

ACTIVITY 7

Prepare for a debate on the topic of 'Shylock: victim or villain?'
a Looking at the three scenes in the assessment task above, list lines in which Shylock is shown as good or bad.
b Think about the performances of Shylock that you have seen and explain how the actor and/or director have made him seem like a villain or a victim.
c Prepare a two-minute speech arguing your point of view, using evidence from the text and the film(s).

In your assessment, you will need to make links between Shakespeare's written work and film, audio or live performances of the same scenes. You will be looking at what Shakespeare wrote and how these scenes have been interpreted by others. When exploring the written text, you need to choose quotations to support your ideas.

ACTIVITY 8

How do the Prologue and Act 1, Scene 1 of the play and the opening scenes of Baz Luhrmann's film prepare the audience for the tragedy of *Romeo & Juliet*? The quotations below are examples you could refer to in your answer.

'civil blood makes civil hands unclean'

'Do I live dead, that live to tell it now'

'star-cross'd lovers'

'O brawling love, O loving hate'

'As I hate hell, all Montagues, and thee'

'Your lives shall pay the forfeit of the peace'

ACTIVITY 9

Read the student response on the right, which looks at the beginning of *The Merchant of Venice*. How would you improve and complete the paragraph?

STUDENT

For a comedy, The Merchant of Venice begins depressingly. Antonio's first line is 'I know not why I am so sad.' This suggests that Antonio is a confused character and Jeremy Irons' performance backs this up. He appears to be waiting moodily for Bassanio.

SHAKESPEARE AND FILM/AUDIO/LIVE PERFORMANCE

Do I need to read the whole play?

Yes. You should aim to read and watch, or listen to, the whole play, so that you understand the complete story. However, the task will ask you to focus on one or two scenes, so make sure that you understand the words, stage directions, characters and events that appear in those scenes.

What should I look for when reading the play?

When reading the play, try to imagine that you are a director. Think about:

- what happens in the scene or scenes
- the words, actions and intentions of the characters
- how the actors say their lines and what they should be emphasizing
- how the actors move
- where each scene is set
- the costumes
- the lighting.

UNIT 1

What should I look for when listening to or watching a performance?

As you watch or listen to the performance, make notes on how the performance compares to your own reading of the scene. Did the actors interpret their characters as you thought they would? Has the play been set in a different place or at a different time?

How should I plan my response?

Before you start to write, think carefully about the bullet points given in the main task. These will help you to plan your answer and help you to check that you have covered all the important details.

HOW TO APPROACH UNIT 1

LITERARY HERITAGE POETRY

What do I need to study?

For this part of Unit 1 you will study **either** 15 poems by one poet chosen from the following:

- Robert Browning
- Thomas Hardy
- Wilfred Owen
- Christina Rossetti
- William Shakespeare

or you will study Chaucer's *The General Prologue to the Canterbury Tales*.

What will the tasks be like?

Two tasks will be set on each poet and you must do **one** of those tasks. The task will ask you to compare two linked, named poems by the poet you have studied. It will include a list of bullet points, suggesting areas that you should write about.

How much should I write?

You will write an essay of up to **1000 words**. You will have about three hours to do this. The writing time may be split across a number of shorter sessions.

How will my response be marked?

You will be marked on the Assessment Objectives listed below.

- **AO1:** You need to show that you understand the texts and have your own ideas about them. You should back up your ideas with quotations from the text.

- **AO3:** You need to find similarities and differences between the two poems and explore them. The links might focus on theme, style, viewpoint and structure.

LEARNING CHECKLIST

In this chapter you will learn to:

1 Respond with insight and imagination.

2 Use quotations to support your ideas.

AO1

Why poets use literary devices

Literary devices are the tools of the poet's trade. They:

- help us **see** images in our minds, through simile, metaphor and personification
- help us **hear** the feeling in the poems through onomatopoeia, alliteration, assonance and rhyme
- shape ideas into **patterns** by using rhythm, rhyme, repetition and set structures.

When writing about poems, think about the literary devices the poet has used. Ask yourself why the poet has used them and what effects they create.

CRASH!

ACTIVITY 1

Remind yourself of the meanings of different literary devices by putting them into a spider diagram like this one.

Underline the key terms, and then write definitions and give examples.

personification: giving something living qualities, e.g. 'the wind whispered'

LITERARY DEVICES

Responding with insight and imagination

Insight means having your own ideas about a poem. The best way to explore a poem is to **annotate** it. Underline the parts you like best and try to work out why they are effective. What does it make you think of? How does it sound? Is it part of a pattern or does it jar?

The poem below describes the harsh weather that soldiers on the front line had to endure during the First World War. Look at how a student has annotated it.

From 'Exposure'
by Wilfred Owen

there are lots of them, one after the other

Sudden successive flights of bullets streak the silence.
Less deathly than the air that shudders black with snow,
With sidelong flowing flakes that flock, pause, and renew;
We watch them wandering up and down the wind's nonchalance,
  But nothing happens.

Pale flakes with fingering stealth come feeling for our faces –
We cringe in holes, back on forgotten dreams, and stare, snow-dazed,
Deep into grassier ditches. So we drowse, sun-dozed,
Littered with blossoms trickling where the blackbird fusses,
  – Is it that we are dying?

Slowly our ghosts drag home: glimpsing the sunk fires, glozed
With crusted dark-red jewels; crickets jingle there;
For hours the innocent mice rejoice: the house is theirs;
Shutters and doors, all closed: on us the doors are closed, –
  We turn back to our dying.

word implies no one cares about the soldiers' suffering

short lines at the end of stanzas makes it sound disappointing and sad

alliteration of 'f' makes the snow sound soft and gentle

word implies cold, but also fear

a word invented by the poet, describing glowing coals

repetition emphasizes how excluded the men feel

When you are writing about poems you need to back up your ideas with quotations. Short quotations are often better than long ones. Remember to use quotations to make points, explaining what effects they create.

ACTIVITY 2

a With a partner choose a poem you are studying and practise annotating it. Note which lines have a strong effect and try to work out why.

b Write a paragraph about the poem, using short quotations and your annotations.

Wilfred Owen's 'Anthem for Doomed Youth' is a **sonnet**. Below is an extract from an early draft of the poem. The final version is in your Anthology.

ACTIVITY 3

Read the list below, which shows the differences between Owen's first draft and final poem. Discuss why you think Owen made the choices he did in his final version.

- The title was originally 'Anthem for Dead Youth'.
- Line 3 originally read 'Let the majestic insults of their iron mouths'.
- 'Orisons' in line 4 is a very old word meaning 'prayers'. Originally Owen wrote 'requiems' and 'priest-words'.
- In line 12, Owen previously included the word 'cheeks' instead of 'brows'.

Poetry by design

Poets are designers because they create a structure and shape for their poems. Some of these designs are unique to individual poems but others are traditional forms.

A sonnet is a traditional poetic form. It has:

- 14 lines of iambic pentameter (where each line has ten syllables)
- a rhyme scheme
- a turn, when the message of the poem changes. In Shakespearean sonnets the turn comes after 12 lines.

'Sonnet 130'
by William Shakespeare

My mistress' eyes are nothing like the sun;
Coral is far more red than her lips' red;
If snow be white, why then her breasts are dun; *a dull grayish brown colour*
If hairs be wires, black wires grow on her head.
I have seen roses damask'd, red and white, *covered with a pattern*
But no such roses see I in her cheeks;
And in some perfumes is there more delight
Than in the breath that from my mistress reeks.
I love to hear her speak, yet well I know
That music hath a far more pleasing sound;
this is where the poem 'turns' I grant I never saw a goddess go;
My mistress, when she walks, treads on the ground:
And yet, by heaven, I think my love as rare
As any she belied with false compare. *contradicted*

ACTIVITY 4

a In this sonnet Shakespeare makes fun of far-fetched love poems by saying that his girlfriend is nothing special. Read the first 12 lines. How do you think she would feel if she read this?

b Read the last two lines. How does his message change here?

People in poetry

Geoffrey Chaucer (1343–1400) wrote in an early form of English, called **Middle English**. *The Canterbury Tales* is about a group of pilgrims travelling to a shrine at Canterbury. The prologue gives a description of these pilgrims.

In the extract below, Chaucer introduces one of the pilgrims, known as the 'yong squier'. Try reading the words aloud to make them easier to understand.

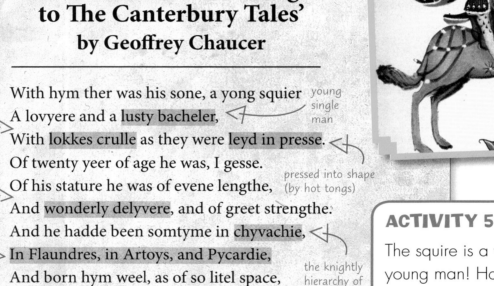

From 'The General Prologue to The Canterbury Tales'
by Geoffrey Chaucer

With hym ther was his sone, a yong squier   *young single man*
A lovyere and a lusty bacheler,
With lokkes crulle as they were leyd in presse.
Of twenty yeer of age he was, I gesse.
Of his stature he was of evene lengthe,   *pressed into shape (by hot tongs)*
And wonderly delyvere, and of greet strengthe.
And he hadde been somtyme in chyvachie,
In Flaundres, in Artoys, and Pycardie,
And born hym weel, as of so litel space,   *the knightly hierarchy of chivalry*
In hope to stonden in his lady grace.
Embrouded was he, as it were a meede   *playing the flute*
Al ful of fresshe floures, whyte and reede.
Syngynge he was, or floytynge, al the day;
He was as fressh as is the month of May.
Short was his gowne, with sleves longe and wyde.
Wel koude he sitte on hors and faire ryde.
He koude songes make and wel endite,   *took great delight*
Juste and eek daunce, and weel purtreye and write.
So hoote he lovede, that by nyghtertale   *poetry*
He sleep namoore than dooth a nyghtyngale.
Curteis he was, lowely and servysable   *he carved meat for his father at dinner*
And carf biforn his fader at the table.

curly hair
well developed
places in France
his clothes were embroidered
jousting
so sociable and active at night
well-mannered

ACTIVITY 5

The squire is a very attractive young man! However, being abroad has not given him time to meet any girls back home. Write his profile for an Internet dating site, including information from the poem.

Emotions in poetry

Poetry is a perfect way to express strong emotions. But if the poet just said, 'I feel sad,' it wouldn't be much of a poem! So writers find ways to express their feelings through imagery to allow their readers to experience the emotions for themselves.

Refer to the poems in your Anthology for the activities on this page.

ACTIVITY 6

In 'The Darkling Thrush', Hardy is feeling depressed. It is the beginning of a new century but nature seems at her lowest point.
  a Underline all the negative words in the poem.
  b Highlight all the words to do with ghosts.
  c Why do you think Hardy brings in the idea of haunting?
  d Something happens to lighten his mood. What is it and how does it affect him?

ACTIVITY 7

Read Rossetti's 'Promises like Piecrust'. Think about the links between the two things being compared.
  a Who might Rossetti be talking to? She seems to be asking someone to stay friends rather than become a lover.
  b What are the links between piecrust and promises?

Irony and unreliable narrators

Irony is saying something different to what you really mean. For example, if someone says, 'What a lovely day!' when it is pouring with rain, he or she is being ironic.

Robert Browning uses irony in his poem 'My Last Duchess'. It is narrated (spoken) by a duke, who is talking about a portrait of his former wife. However, although it is not said directly, it becomes clear that the duke has had his wife killed and is looking for his next wife!

ACTIVITY 8

Read 'My Last Duchess' in your Anthology and underline all the clues which suggest that the duke has had his wife killed.

Some poets use a narrator in their poems. This means that the person who is 'speaking' is a character created by the poet, rather than the poet speaking directly.

In Browning's poem, 'Porphyria's Lover', the narrator is a murderer who tells the story of how he killed his girlfriend. He thinks it is what she wanted, but he is an **unreliable narrator**, which means we cannot trust what he says.

ACTIVITY 9

Read 'Porphyria's Lover' in your Anthology. Write a newspaper article about the murder, creating your own headline and text.

Layers of meaning

Many poems have different layers of meaning. The outer layer is the most obvious but under that there are often other meanings too.

To explore the deeper meaning of a poem you need to look at clues that the poet gives you. Think about what the poet is implying by the choice of words, descriptions and imagery.

For example, in the third stanza of Hardy's poem 'In Time of The Breaking of Nations', the poet refers to a young woman and her boyfriend:

> Yonder a maid and her wight
> Come whispering by:
> War's annals will cloud into night
> Ere their story die.

On the surface, Hardy is talking about a particular woman and man, but underneath he may be talking about all human relationships between men and women.
He is saying that even when historic events such as wars have faded from the records of the past, love will still be important to people.

ACTIVITY 10

In 'During Wind and Rain', Thomas Hardy gives us four snapshots of a family in the same setting. The last two lines of each stanza show the years going by. Read the poem in your Anthology, then draw four pictures, one for each stanza.

LEARNING CHECKLIST

In this chapter you will learn to:

1 Compare and link texts, looking at how different writers express meaning and create effects.

Looking for similarities and differences

In the Assessment you will need to **compare** two poems written by the same poet. This means writing about similarities and differences between them. You should think about:

- how characters are presented; for example, two characters in 'The General Prologue to The Canterbury Tales'
- the feelings described in the poem, such as love, grief, regret or joy
- the situations that the poet writes about, such as fighting in a war or going on a pilgrimage
- the language used, including unusual words, repetition or imagery.

Poems linked by theme

Look at two poems by Wilfred Owen: 'Mental Cases' and 'Disabled'. They are both about the effects of the First World War on young lives.

ACTIVITY 1

Use copies of these poems from your Anthology and put them side by side. With a partner:

a underline words and phrases that show the physical effects of war on the soldiers

b underline words and phrases that show the mental suffering of the soldiers

c write a conversation in which two doctors talk about their experiences with affected soldiers.

UNIT 1

Comparing how characters are presented

The Canterbury Tales were written over 600 years ago but Chaucer makes his characters so real that we can imagine them as people we might meet today.

Think about the Wife of Bath and the Miller from 'The General Prologue to The Canterbury Tales'. With a partner, discuss which famous living people have similar qualities to these characters. Then try the activity below.

ACTIVITY 2

a Sketch each character on a separate piece of paper. Make sure you draw what is described in the text.
- Annotate your drawings with words and phrases from the text.
- Explain what each description tells us about the character. Many of the physical descriptions give clues about the characters' personalities.

b Compare the ways Chaucer portrays these characters.
- Are there similarities in the way Chaucer makes you feel about them?
- Are there similarities in the language he uses to describe them?

Comparing the feelings described

Poems can be linked by the feelings or emotions that a writer describes, even if the situations are different. In the poems 'The Darkling Thrush' and 'Beeny Cliff', Thomas Hardy expresses feelings that swing between sadness and joy. One poem is about hearing a thrush in winter and the other is about his dead love.

ACTIVITY 3

Copy and complete the grids below to help you compare the poems.

a First, select phrases from 'The Darkling Thrush' that show the feelings listed in the first grid below.

Feelings	Quotations
depression	
loneliness	
joy	'full-hearted evensong'
optimism	

b Next look at the quotations from 'Beeny Cliff' in the second grid. Write down the feelings that you think the quotations suggest.

Quotations	Feelings
'...with bright hair flapping free –'	
'The woman whom I loved so'	
'The woman now is – elsewhere –'	sadness
'...and will laugh there nevermore.'	

ACTIVITY 4

Design a mask like the one on the right to show different feelings in one of the poems above. Decorate the mask with suitable quotations from the poem. Include quotations that reveal feelings of both happiness and sadness.

Comparing situations

Even when a poet is writing about similar situations, the effects created by separate poems can be very different. Two of Browning's poems feature a situation where a girl is dead and a man speaks of his love for her.

In the poem 'Evelyn Hope', Evelyn, a 16-year-old girl, has died and the narrator, a man three times her age, visits her bedside, confesses his love and imagines the two of them together in a future life.

In another poem, 'Porphyria's Lover', a poor man is visited by his lover, Porphyria, who is upper-class and wealthy. The narrator knows Porphyria will not give up her lifestyle even though she is in love. At a moment of pure happiness, he strangles her, so she will never leave him.

ACTIVITY 5

a For each poem, create a spider diagram like the one on the right. Add notes to the diagram about:
- the way the situation develops in each poem
- the way each woman is portrayed
- how the poet shows the motives of each man
- what the man's feelings are in each poem.

b How are the situations in each of the two poems similar and different? Use your spider diagrams to help you plan your answer.

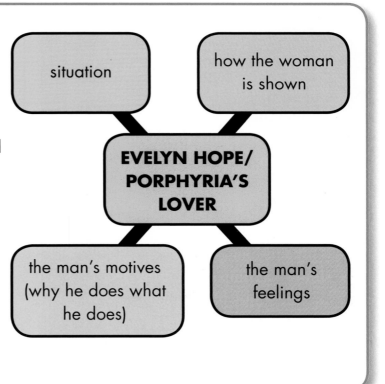

Comparing the use of language

Certain writers may use language in a particular way to give their writing a recognizable style. For example, Christina Rossetti uses fairly simple language but she expresses important, deep ideas.

Look at the poems 'Promises Like Piecrust' and 'Cousin Kate' in your Anthology. Use the list of language features below to help you complete Activity 6.

Language features

- **alliteration** – words that begin with the same sound: 'brittle branches'
- **assonance** – words with similar vowel sounds: 'faded shapes'
- **rhyme** – words with matching end sounds: 'sing/ring'
- **onomatopoeia** – words that sound like what they describe: 'clatter and clunk'
- **repetition**
- **imagery**
- **metaphor** – a comparison where one thing is actually said to be another: 'she is my sunshine'
- **simile** – a comparison using 'like' or 'as': 'she shines like the sun'
- **contrast** – a comparison of different ideas: 'I fell as they advanced'

ACTIVITY 6

Using copies of 'Promises like Piecrust' and 'Cousin Kate':

- highlight examples of language features used in the poems. Try to find examples of at least three different features.
- with a partner, discuss **why** these techniques are used in each poem and what effects they have on the reader.

Writing comparisons

Now practise linking two poems by the writer you are studying by completing the activities on this page.

ACTIVITY 7

Work with a partner.

a Choose two of your set poems and put copies of them side by side.

b Talk about whether the poems are linked by subject matter, situation, character, feelings or language.

c Highlight all the words and phrases that show that there are links between the two poems. Use a different colour to highlight words and phrases that show differences between them.

ACTIVITY 8

a Copy and complete the grid below to help you focus on one similarity and one difference between the two poems. You must include quotations from the poems to support your ideas.

b Repeat the grid to focus on other similarities and differences in the poems.

Points to compare	Poem 1	Poem 2
Identify a <u>similarity</u>.		
Find one quotation from each poem as evidence.		
Find a second quotation from each poem as evidence.		
Explain what the quotations show.		
Identify a <u>difference</u>.		
Find one quotation from each poem as evidence.		
Find a second quotation from each poem as evidence.		
Explain what the quotations show.		

LITERARY HERITAGE POETRY

How many poems should I read?

Even though you will know which two poems you will be comparing, do try to read all 15 poems by your chosen poet or, in the case of Chaucer, the whole of 'The General Prologue to the Canterbury Tales'. This will help you to develop your understanding of the poet's style, themes and subject matter.

Can I discuss the task in class?

Before you start writing your response to the task, you can think about it, discuss it in class and make notes on it. You can check websites and look things up. Your teacher will give you advice about where to find information.

What is meant by 'compare'?

The instruction 'compare' means that you need to pick out features that the two poems have in common and also find differences between them.

How should I plan my response?

Before writing, plan out your response. The plan below shows one possible structure.

Introduction
- Give a summary of the two poems saying what they are about.
- Suggest how the poems are similar or different.

Part 1
- Discuss the first poem in detail.
- Choose quotations from the first poem to support your ideas.

Part 2
- Discuss the second poem in detail, making links to the first poem in order to compare them.
- Refer closely to the language of the second poem, making links to the first poem to compare the language.

Conclusion
- Bring both poems together, saying what their key similarities and differences are.

Can I take the poems into the assessment?

Yes, you may take 'clean' copies of the poems into the Controlled Assessment with you. This means that they should be free from annotations and must not contain any notes.

UNIT 2

Modern Drama

HOW TO APPROACH UNIT 2

What will be assessed in this unit?

In Unit 2 you will study **one** of the following modern plays:

- *The History Boys* by Alan Bennett
- *Hobson's Choice* by Harold Brighouse
- *A View from the Bridge* by Arthur Miller
- *An Inspector Calls* by J.B. Priestley
- *Educating Rita* by Willy Russell
- *Journey's End* by R.C. Sherriff.

How will this unit be assessed?

This unit will be tested by an exam that will last **45 minutes**. In the exam, you must answer **one** question on the play you have studied. There will be two questions to choose from.

The first question will be based on a specific extract. On the Foundation tier paper, this question will include bullet-point prompts to show what you should cover in your answer. The second question will be more general.

There are up to **27 marks** available for Foundation tier answers, which means it is worth 25% of your total English Literature GCSE. Higher tier answers are marked out of **40**.

What should I focus on in my answer?

You will need to show that you understand how drama works. It often involves conflict (disagreement or struggle). The conflict can be between characters, such as Mr Birling and Inspector Goole in *An Inspector Calls*. Sometimes characters have conflict within themselves, such as Hibbert in *Journey's End*. Other plays may show a character in conflict with his or her community, like Eddie Carbone in *A View from the Bridge*.

Think about how an audience might respond to the drama. Would they be amused, horrified, puzzled, or react in some other way? Some dramas involve characters who change as the plot develops, for example, Rita in *Educating Rita* or Willie Mossop in *Hobson's Choice*. You may be asked to focus on specific characters in your answer.

How will my work be marked?

You will be marked on Assessment Objectives 1 and 2.

- **AO1:** You need to show how you respond to the text, using relevant quotations to back up your ideas.
- **AO2:** You need to explain how the writer uses language features, structure and form to create different effects for the reader.

LEARNING CHECKLIST

In this chapter you will learn to:

1 Respond to texts with insight and imagination, using quotations to back up your ideas.

2 Explain how language features, structure and form create different effects for the reader.

Approaching a passage-based question

In your exam you may choose to answer a **passage-based question**. This means that the question refers to an extract printed in the exam booklet. When answering this type of question you will need to know the whole play well, but most of your answer should be focused on the passage.

When approaching a passage-based question:

1 Read the question first.

2 Read the passage at least twice, thinking about:
- who's on stage
- the relationships between the characters, and how they behave and talk
- relevant themes
- any interesting language used
- the use of stage directions
- what happens before and after the passage.

3 Read the question again and think carefully about what you are being asked to do. If it helps, underline key words in the question.

UNIT 2

Understanding key terms

It is important to understand the key terms used when studying literature. Some of these terms may be in the exam questions and you need to be able to use them in your answer.

ACTIVITY 1

Match each key term in the grid below to the correct definition. Look up any terms that you are unsure of. The first one has been done for you.

Key term	Definition
1 insight	**a** how the passage relates to other parts of the play
2 interpretations	**b** the main ideas or issues
3 themes	**c** the general feeling of a passage, e.g. funny, sad or thoughtful
4 setting	**d** the main character
5 protagonist	**e** understanding more than just the surface meaning
6 tone	**f** where the action takes place
7 context	**g** views and opinions, often different

Below are two extracts from different student essays about *Educating Rita.*

STUDENT 1

Opening with a professor in his office, the first scene clearly establishes the idea of education, already flagged up as important in the title of the play.

STUDENT 2

Frank and Rita's opening conversation, which is full of confusion and misunderstanding, creates a sense of humour which interests the audience and makes the opening effective.

ACTIVITY 2

The extracts above relate to **tone** and **theme**. Match each one to the correct key term.

Reading with insight

If you read with **insight**, it means that you have looked below the surface meaning to see the more subtle messages that the playwright is giving the audience. For example, what a character says does not just give direct information, it can also show something about his or her personality, values, mood and relationships.

Read the extract from *Educating Rita*, below. Frank is a university professor speaking to his girlfriend on the telephone.

From Educating Rita
by Willy Russell

Yes? … Of course I'm still here. … Because I've got this Open University woman coming, haven't I? … Tch … Of course I told you. … But darling, you shouldn't have prepared dinner should you? Because I said, I distinctly remember saying that I would be late … Yes. Yes, I probably shall go to the pub afterwards. I shall need to go to the pub afterwards. I shall need to wash away the memory of some silly woman's attempts to get into the mind of Henry James or whoever it is we're supposed to study on this course. … Oh God, why did I take this on?

ACTIVITY 3

What Frank says on the phone reveals a lot about him. Which words below do you think best describe Frank?

patient

sarcastic

professional

loving

short-tempered

hard-working

well-read

patronizing

understanding

educated

disrespectful

old

Supporting your ideas with quotations

When you answer a passage-based question it is important to choose words and phrases from the passage to support your ideas.

ACTIVITY 4

Look at the following quotations. What do they show about Frank? Match each quotation to what it reveals about his character.

Quotation	What is revealed about Frank
1 'But darling, you shouldn't have prepared dinner, should you?'	impatient
2 'some silly woman's attempts'	disrespectful
3 'Tch ... Of course I told you'	unprofessional
4 'whoever we're supposed to study on this course'	regretful
5 'Oh God, why did I take this on?'	patronizing

ACTIVITY 5

Write a short paragraph about what we learn about Frank in the extract on Page 48. Use some of the quotations above to support your answer.

The examiner will want to see you **analyse** the writer's use of language to create certain effects. Good answers will pick out relevant words and phrases from the passage provided and explain **why** they are used.

Read the extract below from *The History Boys*. In this scene, two teachers talk about education and show that they have very different opinions about it.

From *The History Boys* by Alan Bennett

Irwin

[…] I sympathise with your feelings about examinations, but they are a fact of life. I'm sure you want them to do well and the gobbets you have taught them might just tip the balance.

Hector

What did you call them?

Gobbets? Is that what you think they are, gobbets?

Handy little quotes that can be trotted out to make a point? Gobbets?

Codes, spells, runes – call them what you like, but do not call them *gobbets*.

Irwin

I just thought it would be useful…

Hector

Oh, it would be useful… every answer a Christmas tree hung with the appropriate gobbets. Except that they're learned *by heart*.

ACTIVITY 6

Look at the student response below. It explores how language is used in the extract to emphasize two different views on education. Use the words in the panels to fill the gaps.

appreciate

furious

safe

practical

noun

offended

STUDENT

Irwin is _____ about teaching. He wants students to pass their examinations. He clearly does not _____ what Hector does in the classroom. He uses the _____ 'gobbets' to suggest that what he teaches the students is of no real value. Hector is greatly _____ by Irwin's patronizing tone. He is _____ and repeats the term 'gobbets' to show how he cannot believe what Irwin has just said.

Read the extract on the right from *Educating Rita*. Rita is a working-class hairdresser and adult student. She explains why she could not go to a dinner party given by her university tutor, Frank. She explains how she feels divided between two worlds: her working-class background and the new middle-class world of her education.

From *Educating Rita*
by Willy Russell

Rita

I'm all right with you, here in this room; but when I saw those people you were with I couldn't come in. I would have seized up. Because I'm a freak. I can't talk to the people I live with any more. An' I can't talk to the likes of them on Saturday, or them out there, because I can't learn the language. I'm a half-caste. I went back to the pub where Denny was, an' me mother, an' our Sandra, an' her mates. I'd decided I wasn't comin' here again.

ACTIVITY 7

a Look at the language Rita uses in the extract. What does it show us about her? With a partner, talk about:

- her style of speech; for example, colloquial style, choice of words and abbreviations
- what she says; for example, describing what happened on Saturday
- how she expresses her feelings and how she describes herself
- her current situation.

b Now write a paragraph to explain your interpretation of Rita in this passage. Focus on the language she uses and remember to refer closely to the text to back up your points.

You may find some of the following words useful in your answer:

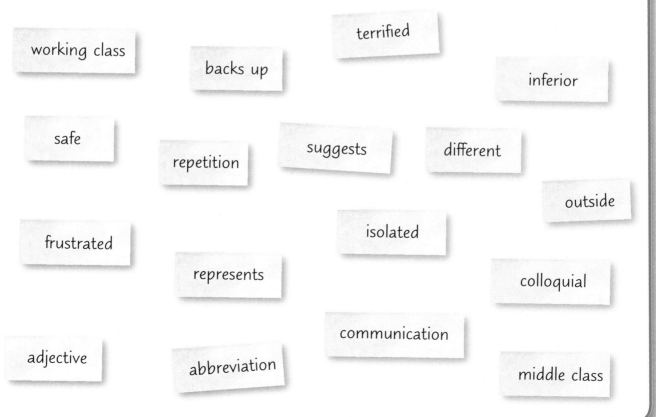

working class

terrified

backs up

inferior

safe

suggests

different

repetition

outside

frustrated

isolated

represents

colloquial

communication

adjective

abbreviation

middle class

LEARNING CHECKLIST

In this chapter, you will learn to:

1 Respond to texts with insight and imagination, using quotations to back up your ideas.

2 Explain how language features, structure and form create different effects for the reader.

Understanding the significance of characters

In your exam, if you answer a general question on the play you are studying, you will need to show a clear understanding of the whole play and of the characters. You will also need to show that you appreciate how the playwright creates and uses characters to represent particular points of view.

Look at the opening and closing lines of an extract from *A View from the Bridge*. This extract was taken from Act One. Read the extract in full in your own copy of the play. In this extract Alfieri, a lawyer from New York, reveals his thoughts to the audience.

From *A View from the Bridge* by Arthur Miller

Opening line

[…]who have I dealt with in my life? Longshoremen and their wives […]

Closing line

[…] and sat there as powerless as I, and watched it run its bloody course.

Some characters do more than just talk with the other characters; some have another purpose like Alfieri in *A View from the Bridge*. Alfieri speaks directly to the audience, giving them background details and setting the tone of the play. In the extract referred to on Page 54, Alfieri introduces many of the key themes.

ACTIVITY I

Find quotations from Alfieri's speech that link to these themes:
- place, i.e. sea and coast
- uncontrollable events
- conflict between family members
- disadvantage
- lawbreaking.

A View from the Bridge is a dramatic **tragedy**. Like many tragedies, the plot involves the death of the main character. There is also a sense of foreboding throughout the play. Foreboding is a feeling that trouble is coming and it is a common feature of tragic plays.

ACTIVITY 2

Look again at the extract referred to on Page 54. Write a paragraph explaining how the extract makes you feel a sense of foreboding. Remember to back up your points with close reference to the text.

Portraying character through language

When writing about your chosen play and its characters, look closely at the playwright's language. Think about the choice of words, phrasing and tone, and their impact on the audience. You need to explain why and how things are said and what this reveals about the characters.

Look at the question below. It relates to a character from Alan Bennett's play, *The History Boys*.

> How does Bennett's portrayal of Mrs Lintott contribute to the dramatic impact of the play?

Here is a student's planned response:

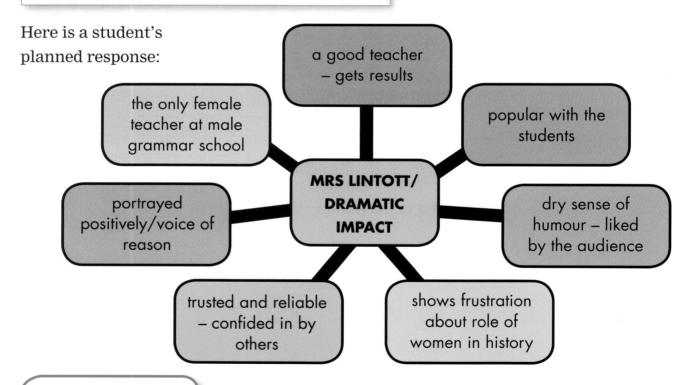

a good teacher – gets results

the only female teacher at male grammar school

popular with the students

portrayed positively/voice of reason

MRS LINTOTT/ DRAMATIC IMPACT

dry sense of humour – liked by the audience

trusted and reliable – confided in by others

shows frustration about role of women in history

ACTIVITY 3

Plan an answer to the same question about a character from the play you are studying. If you are studying *The History Boys*, choose another character from the play.

The student who drew up the spider diagram on Page 56 knows the character and the play well. This means he or she can easily find a quotation to back up a point. Look at the extract from *The History Boys* below, which could be used to back up the point about Mrs Lintott's frustration about the role of women in history:

From *The History Boys*
by Alan Bennett

a game

History's not such a frolic for women as it is for men. Why should it be? They never get round the conference table. In 1919, for instance, they just arranged the flowers then gracefully retired.

went away

History is a commentary on the various and continuing incapabilities of men.

lack of abilities

What is history? History is women following behind with the bucket.

ACTIVITY 4

On the right is a paragraph from a student's answer. It explores Mrs Lintott's 'bucket' metaphor in the extract above. Some key words are missing from the paragraph. Fill in these gaps with words from the panels below.

traditionally

frustrated

powerless

mess

metaphor

STUDENT

Mrs Lintott becomes ____ with her male colleagues and their attitudes. She uses a ____, 'women following behind with the bucket' to suggest that it is men who have ____ made mistakes throughout history and that women are ____ to do anything other than clean up the ____ the men create.

ACTIVITY 5

Choose one feature that you noted about the character in your spider diagram. Write a paragraph explaining it, using a quotation to back up your point.

Character development

If you are answering a question about a character, remember to think about his or her role throughout the play. Characters usually change as the drama unfolds, showing different sides of their personalities. This means that the audience's feelings towards the characters often change too.

Read the extract below. It is from *An Inspector Calls* by J.B. Priestley. Mr Birling, a successful businessman, speaks at a party to celebrate his daughter's engagement. As you read the extract, think about whether or not you like him.

From *An Inspector Calls*
by J.B. Priestley

Just let me finish, Eric. You've a lot to learn yet. And I'm talking as a hard-headed, practical man of business. And I say there isn't a chance of war. The world's developing so fast that it'll make war impossible. Look at the progress we're making. In a year or two we'll have aeroplanes that will be able to go anywhere. And look at the way the auto-mobile's making headway – bigger — *car* and faster all the time. And then ships. Why, a friend of mine went over this new liner last week – the *Titanic* – she sails next week – forty-six thousand eight hundred tons – forty-six thousand eight hundred tons – New York in five days – and every luxury – and unsinkable, absolutely unsinkable. That's what you've got to keep your eye on, facts like that, progress like that – and not a few German officers talking nonsense and a few scaremongers here making a fuss about nothing.

people who spread scare stories

UNIT 2

When you come to write your response, you will need to refer to quotations. It is also important that you explain what the quotations reveal.

ACTIVITY 6

The grid below focuses on Mr Birling. Complete the grid by choosing a suitable quotation to support the point given or by giving a comment and analysis. The first row has been completed as an example.

Point	Quotation	Comment/analysis
mistaken in his views	'a few German officers talking nonsense'	He reads the political situation completely wrong, which calls his judgement into question.
patronizing	'You've a lot to learn yet.'	
egotistical		He feels his status as a businessman makes him important.
likes the sound of his own voice		Repeating himself suggests he likes taking centre stage.

ACTIVITY 7

Choose a key character from the play you are studying and look at one of his or her speeches. Explore how the playwright portrays the character. You may find it helpful to use a grid like the one above.

How can I prepare for this exam?

Make sure that you know the play well. Re-read parts of it from time to time to refresh your memory.

Remember that the play was written to be acted out in front of an audience and not just read. Try to think about how the play might work on stage, how the actors might speak, how they might move and how this might affect the audience.

Should I watch film versions of the play?

There are good film versions of most plays but some do not stick to the original script. For example, the character Denny, who features in the 1983 film version of *Educating Rita*, does not appear in Willy Russell's original play.

What will the passage-based questions be like?

The passage-based question may ask you what is **dramatic** about the extract you have been given. Make sure that you understand what 'dramatic' means.

Passage-based questions may also focus on your reaction to the text as a member of an audience. For example, you may be asked what you find amusing, disturbing, entertaining or moving.

What should I keep in mind when answering passage-based questions?

Remember to look carefully at the **stage directions** as well as at what the characters say. Writers often include stage directions to give instructions about what actors should do and how they should say their lines.

When answering a passage-based question, do not get side-tracked into writing in detail about the rest of the play. You should focus mainly on the extract you have been given.

What will the general questions be like?

General questions may ask you to consider the importance and significance of a particular character, for example, the role of Stanhope in *Journey's End*. You should think about what he or she shows or represents in the play. For example, you could focus on how Stanhope shows leadership through making important decisions about other characters.

Unit 3
Prose from Different Cultures

HOW TO APPROACH UNIT 3

What will be assessed in this unit?

In this unit you will study a prose text from another culture.
It will be one of the following:

- *Of Mice and Men* by John Steinbeck
- *To Kill a Mockingbird* by Harper Lee
- *Anita and Me* by Meera Syal
- *Paddy Clarke Ha Ha Ha* by Roddy Doyle
- *Tsotsi* by Athol Fugard
- *The Joy Luck Club* by Amy Tan.

You may not have much direct experience of the culture that features
in the novel you are studying, but many of the same problems,
issues and dilemmas affect people from all different places and
backgrounds.

How will I be assessed?

This unit will be tested in an exam lasting **45 minutes**. There will
be two questions set on each text, and you must select **one** question
to answer.

This unit is worth 25% of your complete English Literature GCSE.

How will my work be marked?

You will be marked on Assessment Objectives 2 and 4.

- **AO2:** You need to explain how the writer has used language features, structure and form to create different effects for the reader.
- **AO4:** You need to understand the context of your text and the influence of the text on yourself and other readers, including readers from different times and places.

How can I find out about the contexts of my set text?

Reading your set text should give you enough knowledge about the important contexts. For example, in *To Kill a Mockingbird* Harper Lee makes clear how the characters are affected by issues such as prejudice, poverty and views of 'justice'.

You might find that watching a film version helps your understanding of the text. However, remember that the **text** is what you will be examined on and not the film. Sometimes what happens in the film can be different to what happens in the book.

LEARNING CHECKLIST

In this chapter you will learn to:

1 Explain how language features, structure and form create different effects for the reader.

2 Understand the context of your text and explain the influence of the text on yourself and different readers in different places and times.

AO2 & AO4

Choosing a passage-based question

If you answer the passage-based question in the exam, you need to look closely at the extract you are given. You may be asked to explore how the writer portrays a character or presents a theme, or how an event is made interesting for the reader. You will also need to think about how the writer uses language and form to convey ideas.

You need to read the passage through twice and underline <u>key words</u>

Remember, you need to show that you understand **when** the text was written and **where** it is set. Attitudes and values change over time and differ depending on the culture. You could use the steps below to approach a passage-based question.

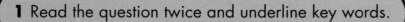
1 Read the question twice and underline key words.

2 Read the extract twice. Underline words and phrases that:
- create a sense of time and place
- show how the characters' attitudes are different from those of today
- show who is telling the story and how they tell it.

UNIT 3

Look at the question below. It is similar to one you might face in the exam. Notice how a student has annotated the question to check what is being asked.

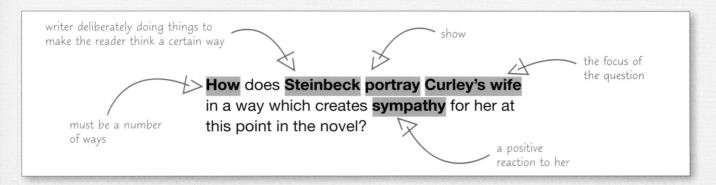

writer deliberately doing things to make the reader think a certain way

show

the focus of the question

How does **Steinbeck** **portray** **Curley's wife** in a way which creates **sympathy** for her at this point in the novel?

must be a number of ways

a positive reaction to her

ACTIVITY I

Add your own annotations to copies of the questions below. Work out what the examiner is asking you to do in each case.

This question is about Meera Syal's novel *Anita and Me*:

> i) How does Syal's writing here vividly reveal that Anita and Meena come from different worlds?

This question is about Roddy Doyle's book, *Paddy Clarke Ha Ha Ha*:

> ii) Explore the ways in which Doyle portrays the relationship between Paddy's parents at this moment in the novel.

Showing awareness of differences

When you write about a text from a different time, you need to show that you understand how the attitudes of the characters in the text are different to those of today. Things that were acceptable in the past may not be so acceptable today. Also, remember that what is acceptable in one country or culture may be offensive in another.

Read the statements below taken from *Of Mice and Men*, a novel set in America during the 1930s.

'I tell ya, you got floozy idears about what us guys amounts to. You ain't got sense enough in that chicken head to even see that we ain't stiffs.'

'I wisht somebody'd shoot me if I got old an' a cripple.'

'They play cards in there, but I can't play because I'm black. They say I stink.'

'Whyn't you get Candy to shoot his old dog… Candy feeds him milk. He can't chew nothing else.'

ACTIVITY 2

Choose two of the statements above and identify the **prejudice** or unfair opinions in them. Now explain how our attitudes today are different.

Language choices and quotations

When you are writing about a text, you need to support the points you make with quotations and discuss them. You also need focus on **how** the writer uses language to create particular effects on the reader; for example, his or her choice of words and imagery.

Read the extract on the right from *To Kill a Mockingbird*.

From *To Kill a Mockingbird* by Harper Lee

Maycomb was an old town, but it was a tired old town when I first knew it. In rainy weather the streets turned to red slop; grass grew on the sidewalks, the courthouse sagged in the square. Somehow, it was hotter then: a black dog suffered on a summer's day; bony mules hitched to Hoover carts flicked flies in the sweltering shade of the live oaks on the square. Men's stiff collars wilted by nine in the morning. Ladies bathed before noon, after their three o' clock naps, and by nightfall were like soft teacakes with frostings of sweat and sweet talcum.

pavements

liquid mud

linked

drooped

light dustings

ACTIVITY 3

Complete the grid below to explore how the author uses language features to create an impression of Maycomb as a town that is past its best.

Quotation	Language feature	Analysis/comment
'a tired old town'		suggests a worn out place
	alliteration	suggests that the heat is unavoidable and stifling
'Men's stiff collars wilted'	metaphor	
	simile	implies the heat spoils the women's attempts to look fashionable

Different social and cultural settings

People's attitudes towards many things vary depending on where and when they live. For example, attitudes towards women in the 1930s were different from those today.

Here are some quotations from *Of Mice and Men*, which is set in the USA in the 1930s. They are all linked to Curley's wife. Some are made by the men working on the ranch and some are spoken by Curley's wife herself; others are made by the narrator.

'a tart'

'I get lonely'

'...I can't talk to nobody but Curley. Else he gets mad.'

'her face was sweet and young'

'I seen her give Slim the eye'

'what a tramp'

'...the discontent and the ache for attention were all gone from her face'

'You got no call foolin' aroun' with other guys, causin' trouble'

'Ain't I got a right to talk to nobody'

ACTIVITY 4

Read the quotations above. Decide which make the reader feel sympathy for Curley's wife and which make the reader dislike her.

When you answer a passage-based question, you need to focus mainly on the extract, but you also need to show that you understand the whole novel.

The text below is from a student's essay about Curley's wife and attitudes towards women at the time. Here, the student shows that she understands not just the passage but also the whole novel and the time and place in which it was written.

ACTIVITY 5

Read the extract from the student's essay carefully and decide which words below fit which gaps. Use a dictionary to look up any words that you are unsure of.

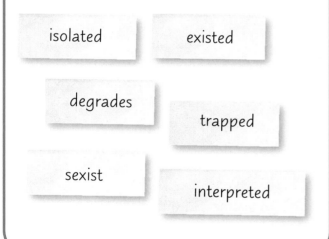

isolated

existed

degrades

trapped

sexist

interpreted

STUDENT

The men on the ranch treat Curley's wife badly. Even her husband talks about her in a way that is disrespectful. As the only woman on the ranch she is an ____ figure. Her flirty nature is ____ by the men as sexual. However, the author is actually presenting a young woman who is ____ in a loveless marriage. She is really trying desperately to make contact with others. Steinbeck uses Curley's wife to reveal the ____ attitudes towards women that ____ in America during the 1930s when the novel was written. He presents a society that sees women as merely sexual objects and which ____ them. Although sexism exists today, there is a much greater sense of equality between men and women.

Different political and historical settings

Novels that are set in the past reflect the history of that period. Writers show the different social and political viewpoints of the time through the characters.

Read the extract below from Athol Fugard's novel *Tsotsi*. The novel is set in a South African township during apartheid (a political system that kept different races apart). The extract describes life in the township, and some of the difficulties that people faced.

From *Tsotsi*
by Athol Fugard

Among those who took their turn in the queue that Sunday afternoon was Miriam Ngidi. She was eighteen years old and carried her baby on her back. When she reached the queue she put down her paraffin tin and prepared herself with a sigh of resignation for the long wait that lay ahead until she reached the tap. It would take her half an hour.

acceptance, because she can't change things

That was one of the things you learnt in the township without ever actually being taught – how to measure the time of a queue by its length. It wasn't as simple as it sounded, a question of so many feet meant waiting so long. The number of buckets and paraffin tins came into the equation. Even the tap itself was a variable. It alternated between a strong, resounding burst of water that hammered onto the bottom of the paraffin tin with a roll like thunder, and a liquid, weak trickle that whispered when it hit the bottom of a bucket and after that flowed silently. There was something of a law to this alternation. It flowed weakest when it was needed most, in the early morning, then again at noon, and at supper time. So unconscious had been the learning of all this that Miriam Ngidi made her calculations without realising it. About three o'clock, maybe thirty people, mostly with one bucket each. She reckoned on half an hour.

working out

loud

something that changed

change from one thing to another

ACTIVITY 6

What do you think Fugard is saying about life for black people in South Africa under apartheid? Write a paragraph which explains your ideas.

You might want to think about:

- what there is a shortage of
- what people have to do.

Make sure that you use evidence from the text to back up your points.

Under apartheid, black people in South Africa were forced by the government to live in separate townships, like the one in the novel. Living conditions were very bad, with limited access to clean water and electricity. Many people around the world campaigned to bring an end to apartheid and the poster on the right was part of this campaign. Apartheid was finally ended in the early 1990s.

ACTIVITY 7

What is Miriam's attitude to her surroundings in the extract? Why do you think she feels like this?

Comment, Criticism and Analysis

LEARNING CHECKLIST

In this chapter, you will learn to:

1 Explain how language features, structure and form create different effects for the reader.

2 Understand the context of your text and explain the influence of the text on yourself and different readers in different places and times.

Commenting on texts

This chapter is about how to answer questions that ask you to comment, evaluate and analyse. For example, you may be asked to **comment** (say how) the author shows the development of a character. You may need to **evaluate** (say how effectively) an author creates an exciting conflict. You may need to **analyse** (explain) how parts of the text have been structured to create effect.

Understanding context

The novel that you will be studying for this unit will be set in a different culture and perhaps a different historical period. You should try to explore its setting, the characters' beliefs and what their communities expect of them.

ACTIVITY I

Look at the descriptions below. Which apply to the novel you are studying?

- set in a country outside the United Kingdom
- set in the United Kingdom, but features characters from a different country
- set more than 50 years ago
- deals with political issues
- deals with social issues
- explores the religious beliefs of the characters
- explores conflict between communities

UNIT 3

Narrative voice

Every novel has a narrator: someone who tells the story.
There are two main types of **narrative voice**, both of
which are described below.

First-person narrator	Third-person narrator
told by a character in the novel: uses 'I/we'	written in the third person: uses 'he/she/they'
may have gaps in knowledge (because they cannot witness everything that happens)	may be omniscient (all-knowing)
tone may be conversational and informal	tone is usually more objective and formal
there may be more than one first-person narrator in a novel (different characters may tell different bits of the story)	there is likely to be only one narrator, who will tell the story throughout

ACTIVITY 2

Read the extracts in the panels. With a partner, decide what type of narrator each one has.

This was terrible; in front of the others, I couldn't sort out my little brother.

Tsotsi feared nothingness. He feared it because he believed in it.

My stomach turned to water and I nearly threw up when Jem held out the blanket and crept toward me.

I do not have many memories of my very early childhood, apart from the obvious ones, of course.

George's voice became deeper. He repeated his words rhythmically as though he had said them many times before.

Characterization

When analysing characters, you should think about how they are described, what they say and how they behave with other characters. Often the main character in a novel will go on an emotional 'journey' that changes them. Look at the flow diagram below. It maps out Paddy Clarke's development in *Paddy Clarke Ha Ha Ha*.

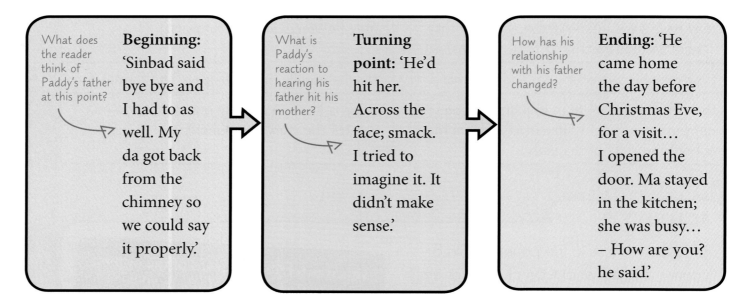

What does the reader think of Paddy's father at this point?

Beginning: 'Sinbad said bye bye and I had to as well. My da got back from the chimney so we could say it properly.'

What is Paddy's reaction to hearing his father hit his mother?

Turning point: 'He'd hit her. Across the face; smack. I tried to imagine it. It didn't make sense.'

How has his relationship with his father changed?

Ending: 'He came home the day before Christmas Eve, for a visit… I opened the door. Ma stayed in the kitchen; she was busy… – How are you? he said.'

Read a student's response below and see if you agree with her analysis of Paddy Clarke's development as a character.

STUDENT

Early in the novel, Paddy's father is shown playing with his children at Christmas, which makes him seem kind. However, there are hints of stress in the family, which Paddy does not understand. When he hears the 'smack', his relationship with his father changes.

At the end, they are like strangers. They talk to each other politely, but not like father and son. Paddy has learned about the adult world and is no longer the same boy.

Setting and culture

Characters are influenced by places. They take on the traditions and values of the country they grow up in. Sometimes they stay in these countries and sometimes they move on.

In *Anita and Me*, Meena's parents have moved from India to the English village of Tollington, but they still love their 'ancestral home' in India.

Read the extract below. It describes Meena's parents' first married home in New Delhi. Think about the questions in the annotations.

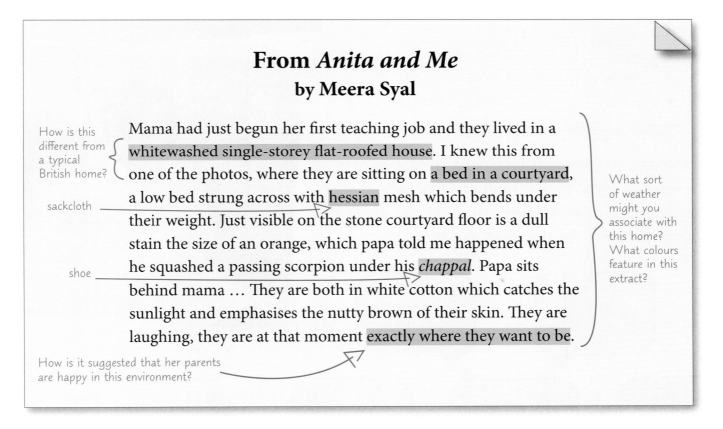

From *Anita and Me*
by Meera Syal

How is this different from a typical British home?

Mama had just begun her first teaching job and they lived in a whitewashed single-storey flat-roofed house. I knew this from one of the photos, where they are sitting on a bed in a courtyard, a low bed strung across with hessian mesh which bends under their weight. Just visible on the stone courtyard floor is a dull stain the size of an orange, which papa told me happened when he squashed a passing scorpion under his *chappal*. Papa sits behind mama … They are both in white cotton which catches the sunlight and emphasises the nutty brown of their skin. They are laughing, they are at that moment exactly where they want to be.

sackcloth

shoe

What sort of weather might you associate with this home? What colours feature in this extract?

How is it suggested that her parents are happy in this environment?

ACTIVITY 3

Choose a passage from the novel you are studying that describes a place that is important in the story.
  a What techniques does the author use to make it vivid?
  b Talk to a partner about the passage. Decide how the place affects the characters in the novel.

Exploring themes

A theme is an important idea that an author explores in a book. There will often be more than one theme. Many of the novels in this unit share the themes of loneliness, isolation and uncertainty.

ACTIVITY 4

Look at the themes below and note which apply to the novel you are studying:
- loneliness
- identity
- childhood
- injustice
- friendship
- education
- prejudice (an unfair opinion).

Some novels are written from a child's point of view and show what it might be like to be that child. The spider diagram below shows how you might explore the theme of childhood.

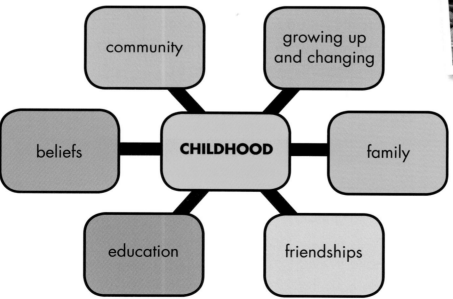

community

growing up and changing

beliefs

CHILDHOOD

family

education

friendships

ACTIVITY 5

Create your own spider diagram exploring a theme in the novel you are studying. Find quotations from the novel to support your ideas.

UNIT 3

Prejudice, injustice and racism

Writers often focus on the difficulties of characters who are treated unfairly due to the colour of their skin, their religious beliefs or simply because they are 'different'. Sometimes a writer wants to make readers aware of injustices from the past or prejudices that exist today.

It is important to look at the social attitudes at the time in which the book is set. For example, in *To Kill a Mockingbird*, Atticus Finch's bravery in representing Tom Robinson is unusual in the American South of the 1930s. In *Tsotsi*, the main character represents millions of black people who suffered under apartheid in South Africa.

ACTIVITY 6

Respond to the following bullet points in relation to the novel you are studying.

- Describe any characters who are treated unfairly because they are 'different' in some way.
- Write down two examples from the novel in which a character suffers from someone else's prejudice.
- How do the characters react to this unfair treatment? Give quotations to support your answer.
- At the end of the novel, who suffers due to the prejudice?
- What point do you think the author is making about prejudice?

Language, structure and form

When writing about your novel, you need to show that you understand how the author uses language, structure and form to put his or her ideas across.

Techniques that authors use include metaphor, simile, alliteration and personification. What techniques do you notice in the extract below from *To Kill a Mockingbird*?

UNIT 3

What impression do we get of the Radley Place?

What technique is used and what does it tell us about the house's appearance?

a porch across the front of the house

What mood does Harper Lee create in this passage?

From *To Kill a Mockingbird*
by Harper Lee

The Radley Place jutted into a sharp curve beyond our house. Walking south, one faced its porch; the sidewalk turned and ran beside the lot. The house was low, was once white with a deep front porch and green shutters, but had long ago darkened to the colour of the slate-grey yard around it. Rain-rotten shingles drooped over the eaves of the veranda; oak trees kept the sun away. The remains of a picket drunkenly guarded the front yard – a 'swept' yard that was never swept – where johnson grass and rabbit-tobacco grew in abundance. Inside the house lived a malevolent phantom.

What technique is used here and what is its effect?

large quantities

ACTIVITY 7

Choose a passage from your novel which uses language in an interesting way. Highlight the words and devices that you think are particularly effective. Now look at how the passage is structured. How does this structure add to the effect?

Bringing together your ideas

Complete the following tasks to show your understanding of language, form and structure, as well as the context of the novel. Remember to use evidence from the text and write about how the author achieves particular effects.

ACTIVITY 8

Choose one of the main characters in the novel you are studying. Explain how his or her feelings and thoughts are expressed at the end of the novel.

To prepare your answer, copy and complete the grid below.

Character's name	Point	Evidence from text
What are the character's feelings and thoughts at the end of the novel?		
How have the character's feelings and thoughts changed?		
How does the author use language to show what the character is feeling and thinking?		
How does the context of the novel influence what the character is feeling and thinking?		

PREPARING FOR UNIT 3

What will the questions be like?

In the exam you will have to answer **one** question, from a choice of two, on the novel you have studied. One question will be passage-based and the other will be more general, asking you to comment, criticize and analyse.

If you choose the **passage-based question**, most of your answer needs to be focused on the extract given. However, you should try to show that you know what happens in the rest of the novel and why the passage given is important.

The more **general question** will expect you to refer to the whole novel. It might trace a particular theme or character throughout the novel.

How long should I spend on my answer?

You have **45 minutes** to answer your chosen question. You should spend some of this time planning what you are going to say.

How will my work be marked?

There are up to **27 marks** available for Foundation tier answers in this part of your assessment. Higher tier answers are marked out of **40**. On the Foundation tier paper, some of the questions may include bullet points that suggest things that you should write about in your answer.

How can I prepare for this exam?

Here are some suggestions that you may find useful:

Make sure you know the text well.

When you've read it two or three times, re-read sections of it again to keep it fresh in your memory.

Find out what sample or past papers look like.

Your exam board, OCR, has prepared sample question papers that your teacher may give you. You can also find them on OCR's website (www.ocr.org.uk).

Look carefully at the type of questions examiners are asking.

Remember that you need to show your knowledge of the context of the text you are studying, even if the question does not ask you about this directly. For example, you may be asked a question on *To Kill a Mockingbird* such as 'What do you find so shocking about the trial of Tom Robinson?' This will be testing your knowledge of the novel and its cultural background.

Remember that you must answer the question.

Don't try to write down all you know about the background of the novel. If you focus on the question you have been asked, what you know will be clear from your answer.

Unit 4

Literary Heritage Prose and Contemporary Poetry

HOW TO APPROACH UNIT 4

How will this unit be assessed?

This unit is tested by an exam. You will answer **two** questions:

- one question on a Literary Heritage Prose text
- one question on **either** a selection of poems by one contemporary poet **or** an unseen poem (that you haven't studied).

The exam lasts for an hour and a half, so you should spend **45 minutes** on **each question**. This unit is worth 25% of your complete English Literature GCSE.

How will my work be marked?

In this unit you will be marked on Assessment Objectives 1 and 2.

- **AO1:** You need to show how you respond to the text, using relevant quotations to back up your ideas.
- **AO2:** You need to explain how the language features, structure and form that the writer has used create different effects for the reader.

You will also be marked on the quality of your writing so make sure that the examiner can read your writing and that your spelling, punctuation and grammar are correct.

What do I need to study?

You will study **one** of the following texts:
- *Pride and Prejudice* by Jane Austen
- *Silas Marner* by George Eliot
- *Lord of the Flies* by William Golding
- *The Withered Arm and other Wessex Tales* by Thomas Hardy
- *Animal Farm* by George Orwell
- *The Strange Case of Dr Jekyll and Mr Hyde* by Robert Louis Stevenson.

What will be in this part of the exam?

You will have to answer **one** question out of a choice of two set on the text you have studied. The first question will be about a specific passage, which will be printed on the question paper. The second question will be more general, referring to the whole text.

How much do I need to know about the background of the set text?

You will **not** be asked directly about the background of your text. However, you will find it easier to understand if you have thought about the time and place in which it is set.

LEARNING CHECKLIST

In this chapter you will learn to:

1 Respond to texts with insight and imagination, using quotations to support your ideas.

2 Explain how the writer uses language, structure and form to present ideas, themes and settings.

Selecting text detail

If you answer the passage-based question in your exam, you should focus on the given passage.

Read the extract from *Pride and Prejudice* below.

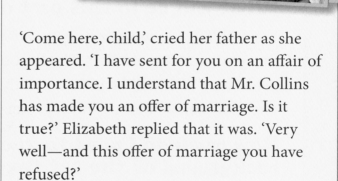

From *Pride and Prejudice*
by Jane Austen

Mr. Bennet raised his eyes from his book as she entered, and fixed them on her face with a calm unconcern which was not in the least altered by her communication.

'I have not the pleasure of understanding you,' said he, when she had finished her speech. 'Of what are you talking?'

'Of Mr. Collins and Lizzy. Lizzy declares she will not have Mr. Collins, and Mr. Collins begins to say that he will not have Lizzy.'

'And what am I to do on the occasion?—It seems an hopeless business.'

'Speak to Lizzy about it yourself. Tell her that you insist upon her marrying him.'

'Let her be called down. She shall hear my opinion.'

Mrs. Bennet rang the bell, and Miss Elizabeth was summoned to the library.

'Come here, child,' cried her father as she appeared. 'I have sent for you on an affair of importance. I understand that Mr. Collins has made you an offer of marriage. Is it true?' Elizabeth replied that it was. 'Very well—and this offer of marriage you have refused?'

'I have, Sir.'

'Very well. We now come to the point. Your mother insists upon your accepting it. Is it not so, Mrs. Bennet?'

'Yes, or I will never see her again.'

'An unhappy alternative is before you, Elizabeth. From this day you must be a stranger to one of your parents.—Your mother will never see you again if you do *not* marry Mr. Collins, and I will never see you again if you *do*.'

The extract deals with two of the novel's main themes:

- family relationships
- marriage.

If you are asked a question about these themes, you need to choose quotations that illustrate them.

ACTIVITY I

Which of the quotations below are most relevant to marriage? Which are most relevant to family relationships? Explain why. Note that some may be relevant to both.

1. Lizzy declares she will not have Mr. Collins...

2. And what am I to do on the occasion?—It seems an hopeless business.

3. Tell her that you insist upon her marrying him.

4. Your mother insists upon your accepting it. Is it not so, Mrs. Bennet?

5. Your mother will never see you again if you do not marry Mr. Collins, and I will never see you again if you do.

Evaluating your quotations

When you include quotations in your answer, you need to explain what they say but also what they **suggest**. For example, in the sentence 'All John's driving skills could not stop the car sliding into the tree' we are told that there was an accident, but the phrase 'all John's driving skills' suggests that he was a good driver who could usually avoid accidents.

Read the passage below from *Silas Marner* by George Eliot.

From *Silas Marner*
by George Eliot

Turning towards the hearth, *fireplace* where the two logs had fallen apart, and sent forth only a red uncertain glimmer, he seated himself on his fireside chair, and was stooping to push his logs together, when, to his blurred vision, it seemed as if there were gold on the floor in front of the hearth. Gold!— his own gold—brought back to him as mysteriously as it had been taken away! He felt his heart begin to beat violently, and for a few moments he was unable to stretch out his hand and grasp the restored *returned* treasure.

The heap of gold seemed to glow and get larger beneath his agitated *worried* gaze. He leaned forward at last, and stretched forth his hand; but instead of the hard coin with the familiar resisting outline, his fingers encountered soft warm curls. In utter amazement, Silas fell on his knees and bent his head low to examine the marvel: it was a sleeping child—a round, fair thing, with soft yellow rings all over its head. Could this be his little sister come back to him in a dream—his little sister whom he had carried about in his arms for a year before she died, when he was a small boy without shoes or stockings? *long socks*

ACTIVITY 2

a Copy and complete the grid below to show what the passage says directly as well as what it suggests. Some examples have been done to help you. Think carefully about what the quotations suggest about Silas's past, his character and his emotions.

Quotation	What it says directly	What it suggests
'...to his blurred vision it seemed as if there were gold on the floor in front of the hearth.'	Silas mistakes the child's golden hair for his missing treasure.	The child is a gift sent to replace his stolen gold. She is something precious.
'The heap of gold seemed to glow and get larger beneath his agitated gaze.'		
'In utter amazement, Silas fell on his knees and bent his head low to examine the marvel...'	Silas looks closely at the child on the floor.	
'...his little sister whom he had carried about in his arms for a year before she died, when he was a small boy without shoes or stockings'		He loved her so much that he took her everywhere with him.

b Choose one quotation from the grid above and write a paragraph explaining the suggested meaning as well as the direct one.

Interpreting a narrator's viewpoint

The narrator's viewpoint is the way a story is told. For example, a first-person narrative will be told through the eyes of one character using 'I' and 'we'. This viewpoint is limited to what one character sees. A third-person narrative will use 'he', 'she' or 'they'. This narrator can 'look inside the head' of different characters.

In *Silas Marner*, George Eliot uses a third-person narrative. Read the extract below about Silas.

From *Silas Marner*
by George Eliot

signs that give warnings about what is going to happen

swellings

mixed

medicine

One day, taking a pair of shoes to be mended, he saw the cobbler's wife seated by the fire, suffering from the terrible symptoms of heart-disease and dropsy, which he had witnessed as the precursors of his mother's death. He felt a rush of pity at the mingled sight and remembrance, and, recalling the relief his mother had found from a simple preparation of foxglove, he promised Sally Oates to bring her something that would ease her, since the doctor did her no good.

ACTIVITY 3

a Pick out the words and phrases that tell us how Silas reacted to Sally Oates.

b What does each word tell us about how Silas feels about her? **Hint:** 'He promised' tells us that he is going to bring her something to make her to feel better because he feels sorry for her.

c What do we learn about the narrator's view of Silas from this extract?

Interpreting an author's use of language

A good writer varies his or her language to create particular effects.
Read the extract below from *Animal Farm*. It describes what happens
immediately after Snowball is forced to leave the farm.

From *Animal Farm* by George Orwell

Silent and terrified, the animals crept
back into the barn. In a moment the dogs
came bounding back. At first no one
had been able to imagine where these
creatures came from, but the problem was
soon solved: they were the puppies whom
Napoleon had taken away from their
mothers and reared privately. Though
not yet full-grown, they were huge dogs,
and as fierce-looking as wolves. They kept
close to Napoleon. It was noticed that
they wagged their tails to him in the same
way as the other dogs had been used to
do to Mr. Jones.

ACTIVITY 4

With a partner, answer these questions, referring to words and
phrases from the extract.
a What does the description of the animals in the first sentence
tell us about them?
b Napoleon took the puppies away from their mothers some time
before this event. What does this suggest?
c What effect is created by the description of the dogs?
d What is suggested by the way the dogs wag their tails?
e How does the final sentence give a clue about what happens
later in the novel?

How language supports ideas, themes and settings

The **way** an author writes is as important as **what** he or she writes. For example, long sentences and detailed descriptions slow the pace of reading and create clear images in the reader's mind. On the other hand, short phrases and strong verbs increase the pace and level of excitement.

Read the two extracts below from *Lord of the Flies*. They describe the death of Simon. Think about which piece of description is slower and which one is faster-paced and more exciting.

moved forward like waves

> At once the crowd surged after it, poured down the rock, leapt onto the beast, screamed, struck, bit, tore. There were no words, and no movements but the tearing of teeth and claws.

curious

> Softly, surrounded by a fringe of inquisitive bright creatures, itself a silver shape beneath the steadfast constellations, Simon's dead body moved out towards the open sea.

steady or fixed

groups of stars

Both extracts link to the theme of good and evil in the novel, looking at:

• savagery versus civilization
• innocence versus corruption.

The setting begins as a paradise but quickly turns into a hell. The author uses the symbolism of dark and light to represent evil/ignorance and goodness/truth.

ACTIVITY 5

a Using a copy of the extracts, highlight all the verbs in each one. Which one has more?

b Use a different colour to highlight all the adjectives in the two extracts. Which one has more?

ACTIVITY 6

Explore the language in these extracts. Work with a partner to complete a copy of the grid.

Words or phrases	Relationship to ideas, themes and setting
'screamed, struck, bit, tore'	These verbs are very violent, suggesting the boys' fear and aggression as they set upon Simon. They are becoming like savages or like the beast. They are losing their innocence.
'the tearing of teeth and claws'	
'inquisitive, bright creatures'	
'the steadfast constellations'	

Another way in which authors use language to support the ideas, themes and setting of a text is through dialogue. Look at the extract from *Lord of the Flies* below.

What characters say and do tells you about their personalities, but it can also move the plot forward. In addition, it can be used to support the themes, ideas and setting in the novel. The conversation between Ralph, Piggy and Simon, below, is relevant to a number of themes and ideas, as well as the importance of the desert island setting.

From *Lord of the Flies* by William Golding

Simon stirred in the dark.

'Go on being chief.'

'You shut up, young Simon! Why couldn't you say there wasn't a beast?'

'I'm scared of him,' said Piggy, 'and that's why I know him. If you're scared of someone you hate him but you can't stop thinking about him. You kid yourself he's all right really, an' then when you see him again; it's like asthma an' you can't breathe. I tell you what. He hates you too, Ralph –'

'Me? Why me?'

'I dunno. You got him over the fire; an' you're chief an' he isn't.'

'But he's, he's, Jack Merridew!'

'I been in bed so much I done some thinking. I know about people. I know about me. And him. He can't hurt you: but if you stand out of the way he'd hurt the next thing. And that's me.'

'Piggy's right, Ralph. There's you and Jack. Go on being chief.'

ACTIVITY 7

Copy and complete the following spider diagram. Add relevant dialogue from the extract on Page 92 to each 'leg'. Explain how the dialogue relates to the theme, idea or setting.

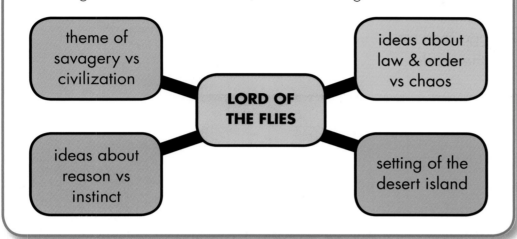

ACTIVITY 8

Write three paragraphs, using your spider diagram as a plan, showing how Golding uses dialogue in the extract to support the themes, ideas and setting. Use the starting points below to help you.

> Piggy says 'He can't hurt you: but if you stand out of the way he'd hurt the next thing. And that's me.' which shows that the only thing that stops Jack turning from civilization to savagery is...

> Simon shows that he knows that Piggy is right about this when he says...

> Ralph's uncertainty when he says 'But he's, he's, Jack Merridew!' shows that...

LEARNING CHECKLIST

In this chapter you will learn to:

1 Respond to texts with insight and imagination, using quotations to back up your ideas.

2 Explain how language features, structure and form create different effects for the reader.

AO1 & AO2

Interpreting an author's meaning

When you interpret any text, you need to show that you understand what the author is saying. This means not just understanding the direct meaning, but also what the author **implies**. This skill is sometimes known as 'reading between the lines'.

Read the extract below from *The Strange Case of Dr Jekyll and Mr Hyde*. Then read the student response on the next page. The response shows that the student has understood the implied meaning as well as the direct meaning.

From *The Strange Case of Dr Jekyll and Mr Hyde* by Robert Louis Stevenson

All at once, I saw two figures: one a little man who was stumping along eastward at a good walk, and the other a girl of maybe eight or ten who was running as hard as she was able down a cross street. Well, sir, the two ran into one another naturally enough at the corner; and then came the horrible part of the thing; for the man trampled calmly over the child's body and left her screaming on the ground.

UNIT 4

Stevenson uses the incident of Mr Hyde trampling over the child to introduce a character who has no conscience. This is shown in the use of the word 'calmly' as though his action doesn't matter to him. The fact that he doesn't stop to see if the girl is hurt shows that he is totally self-centred. He also calls him a 'little man' which implies that he is small-minded as well as short.

ACTIVITY 1

In the extract below, Doctor Jekyll is telling his friend Mr Utterson about Mr Hyde.

> 'Utterson, I swear to God,' cried the doctor, 'I swear to God I will never set eyes on him again. I bind my honour to you that I am done with him in this world. It is all at an end. And indeed he does not want my help; you do not know him as I do; he is safe, he is quite safe; mark my words, he will never more be heard of.'

a Talk about any words or phrases from the extract above that imply something deeper than what is directly said.

b Write a paragraph giving your opinion of what the author is telling us about Dr Jekyll and his relationship with Mr Hyde in this extract.

Interpreting an author's purpose

Most good story writers have something important to say about life or society. This is the **purpose** of the story. George Orwell shows how power corrupts in *Animal Farm*. In 'The Withered Arm' Thomas Hardy shows the destructive effects of the desire for revenge.

As a reader, you have to look for clues that show the author's purpose. In 'The Withered Arm', we are given clues that Rhoda Brook has not forgiven Farmer Lodge for leaving her and that she feels resentful towards his new wife. By the time she realizes she is fond of Gertrude, it is too late and the effect of her 'overlooking' destroys them all.

ACTIVITY 2

Copy and complete the grid below. With a partner, look at these events from 'The Withered Arm' and decide what they show about Hardy's purpose.

Event	What this reveals about Hardy's purpose	Quotation as evidence
first mention of Rhoda		
Rhoda's dream about Gertrude	shows the danger of jumping to conclusions	
Farmer Lodge's reaction to the withering arm	shows how people responded to things that they didn't understand	
the visit to Conjuror Trendle		
the scene with the hanged man		

ACTIVITY 3

Write a paragraph giving your views about what Hardy wanted his readers to learn from this story. Use quotations to back up your points.

Identifying key events in the novel

To make sure you understand the overall structure of your text, draw up a storyboard. This is a summary of the story shown through pictures and captions.

Creating a storyboard can remind you of the key events in the story and help you to understand the **plot**. Think carefully about what happens when and how much time passes between events.

ACTIVITY 4

With a partner, draw up a storyboard for your chosen text.
- Use a grid like the one started below for *Lord of the Flies*.
- Decide on the six most important events in the story.
- Sketch out those events and include captions.
- Add some quotations to link to your chosen events.

We're having a meeting. Come and join in.

(1)

(2) The boys all meet for the first time

(3)

(4)

(5)

(6)

Analysing plot structure

There are two main types of **plot structure**:

- **linear** – where the story moves from the beginning to the end, with events described in the same order in which they happen
- **non-linear** – where events in the story are not arranged in the order in which they happen, but are shown through flashbacks or through clues that hint at what is to come.

An example of a novel with a linear plot is *Pride and Prejudice*. An example of a novel with a non-linear plot is *The Strange Case of Dr Jekyll and Mr Hyde*.

Authors may also use **parallels** in their narratives. This is where some events in the story echo other events. *Animal Farm* includes a parallel in which the ending echoes the beginning. At the beginning of the novel the animals are oppressed by humans; at the end of the novel they are oppressed by the pigs. Orwell uses this parallel to make a point about all people in power being tempted into corruption.

ACTIVITY 5

Read the following extracts from *Animal Farm*. The first is taken from the beginning of the novel and the second is taken from the end. With a partner, discuss how Orwell creates parallels between each point in the narrative.

1 Let us face it: our lives are miserable, laborious and short. We are born, we are given just so much food as will keep the breath in our bodies, and those of us who are capable of it are forced to work to the last atom of our strength.

2 They [the animals] were generally hungry, they slept on straw, they drank from the pool, they laboured in the fields; in winter they were troubled by the cold, and in the summer by the flies.

ACTIVITY 6

a Put these events from *Animal Farm* into the order in which they happen.

the false confessions and the executions of pigs, hens, sheep and others

the sending of Boxer to the knacker's yard

the battle of the cowshed

the pigs walking on their hind legs

Old Major's speech about freedom and equality

drinks and card games with farmers

the battle after the windmill is blown up

b Decide whether *Animal Farm* is a linear or non-linear narrative.

ACTIVITY 7

With a partner, copy and complete the grid below. Use your order of events from Activity 6 in the first column. Discuss possible answers before completing the other two columns.

Event	Actions that caused the event	How actions and events relate to the themes, ideas and setting
Old Major's speech about freedom and equality	Mr Jones's drunken neglect of Manor Farm and Old Major's knowledge that he will soon die	The <u>idea</u> is of a future where animals would get the benefits of their work and would live as equals, sharing everything. The <u>theme</u> is freedom from oppression. The <u>setting</u> makes it possible for the whole community to be present at the speech.

ACTIVITY 8

Use your grid to write two paragraphs.
a Describe the structure of the novel.
b Say how this structure helps to show themes and ideas in the novel.

Interpreting an author's use of setting

The **setting** of a novel or story involves the place, the time and the situation. In *Pride and Prejudice*, the setting is a country village at the beginning of the 19th century. The situation involves a family of girls and their efforts to make suitable marriages.

From *Pride and Prejudice*
by Jane Austen

The village of Longbourn was only one mile from Meryton; a most convenient distance for the young ladies, who were usually tempted thither three or four times a week, to pay their duty to their aunt and to a milliner's shop just over the way. The two youngest of the family, Catherine and Lydia, were particularly frequent in these attentions; their minds were more vacant than their sisters', and when nothing better offered, a walk to Meryton was necessary to amuse their morning hours and furnish conversation for the evening; and however bare of news the country in general might be, they always contrived to learn some from their aunt. At present, indeed, they were well supplied both with news and happiness by the recent arrival of a militia regiment in the neighbourhood; it was to remain the whole winter, and Meryton was the head quarters.

to go there

hat shop

empty

give them something to talk about

found a way

army

ACTIVITY 9

Create a grid with two columns. Copy the quotations in the speech bubbles below into the first column. In the second column, next to each quotation, write what you think Jane Austen is telling us about her setting, and how it affects family relationships and characters.

contrived to learn some from their aunt

amuse their morning hours

well supplied both with news and happiness

a militia regiment in the neighbourhood

duty to their aunt and to a milliner's shop

PREPARING FOR UNIT 4

How should I prepare for the exam?

The best way of preparing for the exam is to make sure that you **read your prose text carefully** and **understand it fully**.

What does 'read it carefully' mean?

This means:

- When you first read the text, try to do it in stages of about an hour at a time. You need to concentrate, without stopping or being interrupted.
- When you feel you know the prose text, keep it fresh in your mind by picking it up from time to time and re-reading part of it for perhaps 15 minutes. Re-read a different part each time.

What does 'understand it fully' mean?

Your first reading of the text should be to find out what happens and what the main characters do. Your second reading gives you the chance to pay more attention to the details. Check the meanings of words and phrases that you are not sure of. You might regret not doing so if they come up in an extract in the exam!

What else should I bear in mind?

You will need to **revise** in the days leading up to the exam. Try to re-read the text. If you feel you already know it well, skim-read some pages. Knowing the text well is vital.

See the film version

You may find it useful to see a film version of the text. Most films follow the text fairly closely, but some do not. For example, the 1954 animated film version of *Animal Farm* ends with the rest of the animals defeating the pigs. This does not happen in the novel. Remember, you are being examined on the **text**, not the film, so make sure you are aware of any differences!

Read the question carefully

In the exam, remember to answer the **question on the paper** in front of you and not one you have practised in class.

HOW TO APPROACH UNIT 4

CONTEMPORARY POETRY

What will this part of the exam consist of?

In this section you will need to answer **one** question.

The question can be **either**:

- on one of the six set contemporary poets

or

- on a single unseen poem (that you have not previously studied).

Here are the six set poets, **one** of whom you might choose to study:

- Simon Armitage
- Gillian Clarke
- Wendy Cope
- Carol Ann Duffy
- Seamus Heaney
- Benjamin Zephaniah.

What will the questions be like?

If you choose to answer a question on a **set poet**, you will have a choice of three questions. The first question will be on a poem printed on the question paper. The second and third questions will ask you to comment on, criticize and analyse one poem from a choice of two poems by the poet you have studied.

If you choose to answer a question on an **unseen poem**, the poem will be printed on the question paper and you will be asked to comment on, criticize and analyse it.

What is contemporary poetry?

Contemporary poetry is poetry written by poets alive today. They often write about recent and current events and issues. For example, Simon Armitage's poem 'The Convergence of the Twain' is about the crashing of aircraft into New York's World Trade Centre on 11th September 2001. Gillian Clarke's poem 'On The Train' touches on the fear of train crashes like the one at Hatfield in the year 2000.

Before you start your studies, your teacher will decide with you whether you will study one of the set contemporary poets or focus on learning skills that would help you to write with understanding about almost any contemporary poem you might come across.

LEARNING CHECKLIST

In this chapter you will learn to:

1 Respond to texts with insight and imagination, using quotations to support your ideas.

2 Explain how the writer uses language, structure and form to present ideas, themes and settings.

AO1 & AO2

Reading and responding to poetry

Poetry is like chocolate: it is very rich and intense. Poets choose their words carefully to create pictures in your mind and to inspire you to think about the ideas they raise. When you read a good poem, it should have an effect on you. You may find things that move you or make you smile.

The diagram below suggests things to think about when reading a poem.

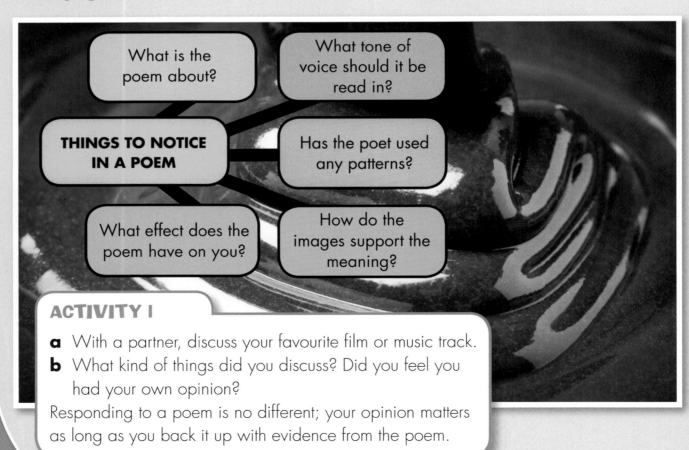

What is the poem about?

What tone of voice should it be read in?

THINGS TO NOTICE IN A POEM

Has the poet used any patterns?

What effect does the poem have on you?

How do the images support the meaning?

ACTIVITY I

a With a partner, discuss your favourite film or music track.

b What kind of things did you discuss? Did you feel you had your own opinion?

Responding to a poem is no different; your opinion matters as long as you back it up with evidence from the poem.

How poets choose words

In your exam you will need to comment on words that the poet uses.

ACTIVITY 2

a Imagine you are writing the poem on the right. Decide which words you would use to fill the gaps.

b Read out your version of the poem. Look at Heaney's version in your Anthology and compare your choices to his. (Note that this is just part of the poem.)

c What do you notice about the rhyme patterns?

From 'Blackberry-Picking'
by Seamus Heaney

Late August, given heavy rain and _____

For a full week, the blackberries would ripen.

At first, just one, a glossy purple clot

Among others, _____, _____, hard as a _____.

You ate that first one and its flesh was sweet

Like _____ _____: summer's blood
     was in it

Leaving stains upon the tongue and _____ for

Picking. Then red ones _____ up and that hunger

Sent us out with milk-cans, pea-tins, jam-pots

Where briars scratched and wet grass _____
     our boots.

Connotations are extra suggestions that words have for readers. For example, the mention of blood and clots carry connotations about injury and death. The scratching briars hint at something threatening. Heaney is preparing us for the second stanza by suggesting that something will go wrong.

Understanding imagery

We all use metaphors. Have you ever had your 'head in the clouds'? That means you are not paying attention. We all use similes. If you say he/she has 'a face like thunder', you mean that someone looks angry.

Poets often use metaphors and similes to show their feelings. Gillian Clarke's poem, 'My Box', is a love poem dedicated to her husband and the life they have shared together. Read 'My Box' in your Anthology.

ACTIVITY 3

a Using a copy of the poem, underline all the words that make the box sound precious.

b The box is a metaphor. What does it represent? What does it show about the writer's feelings?

ACTIVITY 4

Write your own poem called 'My Box'.

a In the first stanza, describe your box. It might be a titanium box or a gold casket. Include where you got it from or who made it for you.

b In your second stanza, write about all the things you would put in your box. Describe things in detail, for example, 'the sunset over the River Mersey in autumn'.

c In your last stanza, write about where you keep your box and what might happen to it in the future.

Reading the clues

Poets often avoid giving direct information. Instead they give clues and ideas, leaving readers to build up their own pictures.

ACTIVITY 5

If a stranger were to look in your schoolbag, what would they find out about you? Discuss this with a partner.

In the panels below are some quotations from 'About His Person' by Simon Armitage. This poem portrays a man and an event, just by noting things that the man carries and the appearance of his hands.

'A brace of keys'

'a rolled up note of explanation'

'an analogue watch, self-winding, stopped'

'A giveaway photograph stashed in his wallet'

'Five pounds fifty in change, exactly'

'a pocket-size diary slashed with a pencil'

'a ring of white unweathered skin'

ACTIVITY 6

a Using the quotations in the panels, write a brief description of the person who owns these things.

b Read the complete poem 'About His Person' in your Anthology. Were your ideas on the right lines?

c Using a copy, highlight words that suggest death or endings; for example, 'expiry'. What do you think happened to this man? What hints can you find in the poem to suggest why this may have happened?

Interpreting the poet's subject matter: experiences of school

School is an experience shared by most people. Although this experience has changed a little since Carol Ann Duffy went to school in the 1960s, you will recognize many of the things she includes in her poems. 'In Mrs Tilscher's Class' is about primary school.

At that time, children at primary school were given small bottles of milk at break, teachers wrote with chalk, and bells were old-fashioned ones rung by hand. Brady and Hindley, who are both mentioned in Duffy's poem, were notorious child murderers convicted in 1966.

ACTIVITY 7

Read 'In Mrs Tilscher's Class' in your Anthology.

a In the first stanza, do you think the children understand what they are learning?

b In the second stanza, how does Duffy show her positive attitudes towards school?

c Why do you think Duffy refers to Brady and Hindley in the second stanza?

d Think about the main themes of the poem. How are the tadpoles linked to this?

e How does Mrs Tilscher finally disappoint Duffy?

f How does Duffy use language to appeal to the senses?
Hint: think about the adjectives that she uses.

During Duffy's schooldays, secondary school was much more formal than it is now and the teachers were often very strict. The school described in 'The Good Teachers' is a secondary school and seems to be a girls' school from which the speaker longs to escape.

ACTIVITY 8

Read 'The Good Teachers' in your Anthology.

a Which subjects does the speaker like? Which does she dislike? Give evidence from the poem to support your ideas.

b The speaker in this poem is rather rebellious. How does Duffy suggest this through her word choices? Give three examples.

c How is the student contrasted with the teachers in the poem? **Hint:** look at the descriptions of their clothes.

d Which teachers do you think the speaker thinks are 'the good teachers'? Use quotations to help you to explain why.

A **parody** is a humorous copy of the style of someone or something. Some poets use parody to write new, amusing poems that echo the originals.

Read the poems below. The first poem is the popular Victorian poem by Jane Taylor. The poem below it is a parody of it by Lewis Carroll. Notice how Carroll has kept the rhythm of the original as well as some of the words and rhyme patterns, but he has changed the subject to a more comic one.

Twinkle, twinkle, little star,
How I wonder what you are!
Up above the world so high,
Like a diamond in the sky.

Twinkle, twinkle, little bat!
How I wonder what you're at!
Up above the world you fly,
Like a tea-tray in the sky.

Wendy Cope has written various parodies, which you can find in your Anthology. 'Sonnet 55', below, is a sonnet by William Shakespeare. Cope chooses to parody this in her poem 'iv', which she presents as one of Strugnell's sonnets. James Strugnell is a character invented by Wendy Cope. He is a bad poet and she uses him to parody the process of writing poetry.

'Sonnet 55'
by William Shakespeare

gold covered

gravestones

conflicts

the god of war

Not marble, nor the gilded monuments
Of princes shall outlive this pow'rful rhyme,
But you shall shine more bright in these contents
Than unswept stone besmeared with sluttish time.
When wasteful war shall statues overturn,
And broils root out the work of masonry,
Nor Mars his sword, nor war's quick fire shall burn
The living record of your memory.
'Gainst death, and all oblivious enmity
Shall you pace forth, your praise shall still find room,
Even in the eyes of all posterity
That wear this world out to the ending doom.
So, till the judgment that yourself arise,
You live in this, and dwell in lovers' eyes.

covered in moss and dirt

stonework

destruction which leads to people becoming forgotten

future generations

ACTIVITY 9

Look at 'Strugnell's Sonnets (iv)' in your Anthology.

a How has Cope changed the words but kept the rhyme and rhythm to create humour in her poem? Make a list of all the changes.

b Has Cope changed the meaning of the poem? How has it moved from being a serious poem to a parody?

LEARNING CHECKLIST

In this chapter you will learn to:

1 Respond to texts with insight and imagination, using quotations to support your ideas.

2 Explain how the writer uses language, structure and form to present ideas, themes and settings.

AO1 & AO2

Themes in poetry

Some poems seem to have an obvious subject (main idea), but there is often a more complicated **theme** behind it. For example, the subject of Seamus Heaney's poem 'Follower' is about being a small boy wanting to be like his father, but it also has the theme of the cycle of life. The subject of Duffy's 'Dream of a Lost Friend' is nightmare, but its overall theme is bereavement and loss.

ACTIVITY I

The quotations in the boxes below are from poems in your Anthology. Match them up to the relevant themes listed beneath.

1 'a ring of white unweathered skin'

2 'Between my finger and my thumb/The squat pen rests./I'll dig with it.'

3 'I've never dreamt of being white/But I can't bear being abused'

4 'You roll the waistband/of your skirt over and over, all leg, all/dumb insolence, smoke-rings.'

5 'I hear your words,/they play inside my head like broken chords.'

prejudice   rebellion   arguing   writing poetry   divorce

Using poetry to protest

Poetry is a great way to express protest. To make a strong point, poets may use repetition and rhymes to make the message stick in the reader's mind. The letters **p**, **d** and **b** are strong consonants. These sounds can add weight to an argument. Think about some angry words in the English language and you will see why.

In 'Bought and Sold', Benjamin Zephaniah complains about the way writers seem to be tamed by the lure of fame. Zephaniah himself has turned down many honours.

ACTIVITY 2

a Read the poem 'Bought and Sold' in your Anthology. Using a copy, underline all the negative words. What effect do they have on you?

b Label the rhyme scheme. How does this pattern and structure add to the impact of the poem?

c List all the words that include **p**, **b** or **d** sounds. Write a paragraph explaining why you think Zephaniah chooses to use these words.

Reading between the lines

Wendy Cope is a poet who likes to have fun with words. In 'Reading Scheme', she uses a form called a **villanelle**. Villanelles have repeated lines at the end of every other stanza and at the end of the poem. Cope uses this form to poke fun at the repetitive style of books from reading schemes, designed to teach young children how to read.

'Reading Scheme' is funny because Cope's story is very different to the ones found in real children's books. On the surface everything sounds fine, but reading between the lines reveals a different story. 'The milkman likes Mummy. She likes them all' implies that 'Mummy' is unfaithful, and not only with the milkman. Jane and Peter are spying on them when 'Daddy' returns home unexpectedly and 'looks very cross'. He may have a gun. The milkman makes a rapid getaway over the wall.

ACTIVITY 3

Re-read 'Reading Scheme' in your Anthology with a partner.
a On a copy, highlight all the phrases that have a double meaning. Be prepared to explain the two meanings.
b Look at the structure of the poem. There are two sets of repeated lines. Circle them in two different colours.
c If you were writing a villanelle called 'Reading Scheme', what subject might you choose and what repeated lines would you include? Remember that the subject should seem suitable for young children, even if reading between the lines reveals a different story.

Writing with a persona

When poets use the first person, 'I', it does not mean that they are speaking as themselves. They may be exploring what it is like to be someone else. This is called taking on a **persona**.

Carol Ann Duffy wrote 'Stealing' after reading a newspaper article about a stolen snowman. The thief in her poem steals other items too, including a bust of Shakespeare. The poem is written from the thief's point of view.

ACTIVITY 4

a Look up 'Stealing' in your Anthology and read it aloud. What sounds are repeated throughout the poem? Back up your ideas with examples.

b How does Duffy make the thief sound scary? Explain your ideas, using quotations.

c Does Duffy create sympathy for this person and, if so, how? Think about the way she suggests that the thief feels like a failure.

d Does the poem tell the reader **why** the thief steals?

The theme of nature

Nature has long been a favourite theme in poetry. Although it is all around us, we struggle to understand it fully. Nature can be very beautiful, but it can also be miserable and dangerous. Seamus Heaney explores the darker side of nature in some of his poems.

Heaney's poem 'Death of a Naturalist' is about a memory. Heaney remembers how, as a boy, he was frightened of frogs, which he imagined were seeking revenge on him for all the tadpoles he had collected.

ACTIVITY 5

a Read 'Death of a Naturalist' in your Anthology. On a copy, highlight all the negative words. What effect do these create?

b Heaney recreates the sound of the frogs with **onomatopoeia**, or words that sound like what they describe, like 'slap'. List all the examples that you can find.

  How does this add to the impact of the poem?

c Why do you think the poem is called 'Death of a Naturalist'? **Hint:** think about the effect of the events in the poem on Heaney as a child.

Poetry and the wider world

Poets often have strong views about things that are happening around them.

Heaney's poem 'Punishment' is about an ancient body dug up from a peat bog. He sees similarities between the fate of this woman, who was accused of adultery, and women who were 'tarred and feathered' by other women if they had relationships with British men during the Troubles in Northern Ireland in the 1970s.

ACTIVITY 6

Read 'Punishment' in your Anthology.

a With a partner, talk about the feelings Heaney creates in the reader:
- towards the young girl
- towards himself.

b An example of a student's response is given below. Try to improve it and add to it. You could focus more on:
- the language in the poem
- the structure of the poem.

Remember to back up the points you make with evidence (quotations) from the poem.

STUDENT

Heaney describes the body of a young girl who was hanged, using natural metaphors: 'a barked sapling'. This suggests how young she is, as well as the colour of the corpse. He makes us feel sorry for her by addressing the girl halfway through, describing her 'before they punished' her as 'beautiful'.

LEARNING CHECKLIST

In this chapter you will learn to:

1 Respond to texts with insight and imagination, using quotations to support your ideas.

2 Explain how the writer uses language, structure and form to present ideas, themes and settings.

How to approach an unseen poem

If you answer the unseen poem question, you will need to look at how language and structure support the meaning of the poem. You also need to back up your ideas with quotations from the text.

In the exam, read the poem at least twice and think about **what** the poet is saying and **how** he or she is saying it. Look at the annotations that have been added to the extract from a poem on the right.

From 'How to Capture a Poem'
by Angela Topping

imperative verb tells reader to focus at start of stanzas

Look for one at midnight
on the dark side of a backlit angel
or in the space between a sigh
and a word. Winter trees, those
elegant ladies dressed in diamonds
and white fur, may hide another.

implies a poem is a wild animal

metaphor creates an interesting image

onomatopoeia brings sounds to life

Look for the rhythm in the feet
of a waltzing couple one, two, three-ing
in an empty hall, or in the sound
of any heartbeat, the breath of a sleeper,
the bossy rattle of keyboards in offices,
the skittering of paper blown along.

UNIT 4

Practising annotation

Making notes around the poem is a good way to explore it. Add comments in the margins, including question marks for parts you don't understand. Circle words you like and imagery that you find particularly striking.

You can annotate the poem during the exam to help you focus your thoughts before you start writing about it.

ACTIVITY 1

Read the poem 'Nettles' below.

a Add your own annotations to a copy of the poem.

b Highlight all the words that relate to anger.

c What impression does this give of the speaker in the poem, and of his relationship with his son?

'Nettles'
By Vernon Scannell

My son aged three fell in the nettle bed.
'Bed' seemed a curious name for those green spears,
That regiment of spite behind the shed:
It was no place for rest. With sobs and tears
The boy came seeking comfort and I saw
White blisters beaded on his tender skin.
We soothed him till his pain was not so raw.
At last he offered us a watery grin,
And then I took my billhook, honed the blade
And went outside and slashed in fury with it
Till not a nettle in that fierce parade
Stood upright any more. And then I lit
A funeral pyre to burn the fallen dead,
But in two weeks the busy sun and rain
Had called up tall recruits behind the shed:
My son would often feel sharp wounds again.

Selecting quotations

When writing about poetry, it is important to provide evidence for your ideas. This evidence should be quotations from the poem. The quotations can be short; even single words put into your own sentences can be very effective. Remember to comment on quotations and to link each one to the point you wish to make.

Below is part of a student's response to 'Nettles'.

STUDENT

'Nettles' is about an incident where the speaker's son got hurt falling into a nettle patch. The words that the poet uses, such as 'spears', 'spite' and 'pain' show how painful the event was. This makes the father want to protect his child from this ever happening again, which he does by taking out his 'fury' on the nettles. This makes the reader feel as if he is a good father for wanting to protect his child.

ACTIVITY 2

With a partner, discuss how you might add to this response. Look back at the poem and think about:
- the last line – what does this suggest?
- the hidden meaning as well as the direct meaning.

Free verse

Free verse is a form of poetry that has no fixed pattern; it does not have a regular beat or a set rhyme scheme. Poets often use poetic devices in free verse, and the choice of every word and its position in the poem is still very carefully thought-out.

ACTIVITY 3

a Read the free verse poem 'Early in the Morning' by Li-Young Lee and the annotations around it.

b Add more annotations of your own to a copy of the poem. For example, pick out words or images that you find powerful.

c Comment on how Li-Young Lee creates sound patterns within the poem without using a fixed rhyme scheme. **Hint:** look for examples of alliteration, onomatopoeia and enjambment (run-on lines), and think about what effects they create.

'Early in the Morning'
by Li-Young Lee

While the long grain is softening
in the water, gurgling
over a low stove flame, before
the salted Winter Vegetable is sliced
for breakfast, before the birds,
my mother glides an ivory comb
through her hair, heavy
and black as calligrapher's ink.

She sits at the foot of the bed.
My father watches, listens for
the music of the comb
against hair.

My mother combs,
pulls her hair back
tight, rolls it
around two fingers, pins it
in a bun to the back of her head.
For half a hundred years she has done this.
My father likes to see it like this.
He says it is kempt.

But I know
it is because of the way
my mother's hair falls
when he pulls the pins out.
Easily, like the curtains
when they untie them in the evening.

delicate words used to set a quiet scene

line break after 'heavy' accentuates the weight

simile suggests the beauty of her hair

line break creates suspense

run-on lines suggest fluidity

simile shows the privacy and beauty of love between older people

opposite of unkempt, his father's joke

Using literary terms

Literary terms provide the vocabulary for commenting on language. It is important that you understand literary terms and that you are confident about using them. They are part of the poet's toolbox.

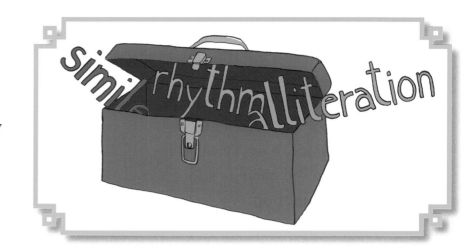

ACTIVITY 4

Below is a grid to help you revise literary terms. Match each term on the right to the correct row in the grid. The grid gives an explanation of each device with examples and a description of its effects.

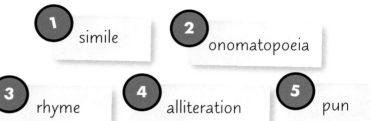

1 simile

2 onomatopoeia

3 rhyme

4 alliteration

5 pun

	Explanation	Examples	Effects
A	words that sound like the thing they describe	splash, bang, thud, whizz, screech, crack, crisp, flutter, scream	engages the reader's senses and makes descriptions more realistic
B	words beginning with the same letter	'dulls to distance all we are' 'my type-writer tapping under stars'	emphasizes words; can help create sound and rhythm in a poem or add to an overall mood
C	humorous use of a word which has more than one meaning	'having done that, Thou hast done' (In this quotation, the poet John Donne creates a pun on his own name.)	shows a poet's cleverness; can make a point or amuse the reader; creates deeper layers of meaning
D	a similar sound in the endings of words	wealth – health	can make a poem more memorable; adds to rhythm; can be used for emphasis
E	a comparison between two things using 'like' or 'as'	'like a little dog, I followed her'	helps you to see how a poet imagines things; can be used to convey emotions

Poem to discuss

Now you have the chance to practise the skills you have developed in this chapter by working with the poem, 'Silence', by Edward Lucie-Smith on the right.

ACTIVITY 5

Read the poem 'Silence'. Discuss what you like about it and what interests you. In particular, consider:

- what the noises in the poem are
- what 'your own noisy machine' is. **Hint:** it's part of your body that you can't live without.
- what 'silence' means in the last line of the poem.

'Silence'
by Edward Lucie-Smith

Silence: one would willingly
Consume it, eat it like bread.
There is never enough. Now
When we are silent, metal
Still rings upon shuddering
Metal; a door slams; a child
Cries; other lives around us.

But remember, there is no
Silence within; the belly
Sighs, grumbles, and what is that
Loud knocking, that summoning?
A drum beats, a drum beats. Hear
Your own noisy machine, which
Is moving towards silence.

CONTEMPORARY POETRY

When preparing for the exam, think carefully about the skills you will be assessed on.

Respond to texts with insight and imagination

You need to show that you understand what a poem is about. You should explain what ideas the writer is putting forward and his or her point of view. Ask yourself questions about the poet's purpose. For example, is the poet trying to shock you into agreeing with his or her attitude to war?

Select text detail to support interpretations

You need to back up your ideas with details from the poem. Examiners often remind you to do this, ending many poetry questions with 'Remember to refer closely to the words and phrases the poet uses'.

Language, structure and form

You will need to keep these aspects in mind when you are preparing to write about poetry. Poems are shorter than plays and novels, so poets need to choose their words with special care. They also need to think carefully about the structure and form of their poems.

Reading poems

The more poems you read, the more familiar you will become with the way poets use language and the effects they want to create. Take time to read all the poems in your Anthology. Think about what you've read and why you enjoyed particular poems.

Writing about a poem in the exam

If you're studying 15 poems by one poet in your Anthology, **do study them all carefully**. Don't miss any out – they may be the ones that appear in your exam!

Structuring your answer

Here is one basic structure you might find helpful to follow:

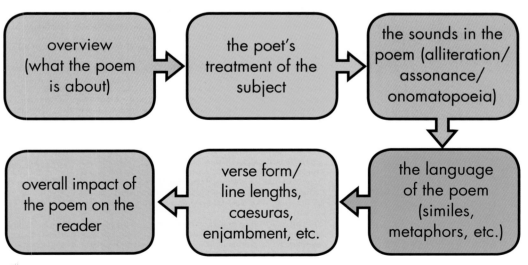

OXFORD
UNIVERSITY PRESS

Oxford University Press is a department of the University of Oxford. It furthers the University's objective of excellence in research, scholarship, and education by publishing worldwide in

Oxford   New York

Auckland   Cape Town   Dar es Salaam   Hong Kong   Karachi
Kuala Lumpur   Madrid   Melbourne   Mexico City   Nairobi
New Delhi   Shanghai   Taipei   Toronto

With offices in

Argentina Austria Brazil Chile Czech Republic France Greece
Guatemala Hungary Italy Japan South Korea Poland Portugal Singapore
Switzerland Thailand Turkey Ukraine Vietnam

Oxford is a registered trade mark of Oxford University Press
in the UK and in certain other countries

© Oxford University Press 2011

Authors: D. C. Coleman, Annie Fox, Garrett O'Doherty, Alison Smith, Angela Topping, Carmel Waldron

The moral rights of the authors have been asserted.

Database right Oxford University Press (maker)

First published 2011

British Library Cataloguing in Publication Data
Data available
ISBN: 978-0-19-832948-0

10 9 8 7 6 5 4 3 2 1

Printed in Spain by Cayfosa-Impresia Ibérica.

Acknowledgements

The publisher and authors would like to thank the following for their permission to reproduce photographs and other copyright material:

p10: Donald Cooper/Photostage; **p11**: Alastair Muir/Rex Features; **p12**: Kean Collection/Staff/ Hulton Archive/Getty Images; **p14**: Roman Sigaev/Shutterstock; **p16**: Everett Collection/ Rex Features; **p17**: Buena Vist/Everett/Rex Features; **p18l**: 20thC.Fox/Everett/Rex Features; **p18r**: themoviestorecollection.com; **p19t**: Sonypics/Everett/Rex Features; **p19b**: Robbie Jack/ Corbis; **p21t**: Columbia/The Kobal Collection; **p21b**: The Everett Collection/Rex Features; **p22t**: Sony Pics/Everett/Rex Features; **p22b**: Sony Pics/Everett/Rex Features; **p29**: Ronfromyor/Stockxpert; **p30**: First World War Poetry Digital Archive; **p31**: Christie's Images/Corbis; **p32**: Ellesmere Manuscript, facsimile edition, 1911, English School, (15th century) (after)/Private Collection/The Bridgeman Art Library; **p33**: Andrew Park/ Shutterstock; **p35**: Fine Art Photographic Library/Corbis; **p36**: Lebrecht Music & Arts Photo Library/Photolibrary; **p37t**: Mary Evans Picture Library/Photolibrary; **p38**: teolin/ Shutterstock; **p39**: Rothenstein, Sir William(1872-1945)/Private Collection/Whitford & Hughes, London, UK/The Bridgeman Art Library; **p40**: Lebrecht Music & Arts Photo Library/ Photolibrary; **p47**: Photostage; **p49**: Acorn Pictures Ltd/The Kobal Collection; **p50**: Alastair Muir/Rex Features; **p51**: woodsy/Shutterstock; **p52**: Acorn Pictures Ltd/The Kobal Collection; **p53**: ITV/Rex Features; **p54**: Michal Daniel, 2008/Guthrie Theatre; **p55**: Michal Daniel, 2008/Guthrie Theatre; **p56**: Fox Searchlight/The Kobal Collection; **p58t**: FPG/Staff/The Hulton Archive/Getty Images; **p58b**: The Mariners' Museum/Corbis; **p59t**: Paul Lovelace/ Rex Features; **p59b**: Dixon, Henry (1820-1892)/S.P.R.O.L. Collection/City of London; **p65**: BBC Films/Film Council/The Kobal Collection; **p66**: Orientaly/Shutterstock; **p68**: The Ronald Grant Archive; **p70**: Alain Nogues/Sygma/Corbis; **p71t**: Miramax/Everett/Rex Features; **p71b**: Radu Sigheti/Reuters; **p72**: The Ronald Grant Archive; **p76t**: Carly Rose Hennigan/ Shutterstock; **p76b**: Image Souce/OUP; **p77**: Universal/The Kobal Collection; **p78**: Mark Winfrey/Shutterstock; **p79**: Miramax/Everett/Rex Features; **p84**: Capital Pictures; **p85**: The Ronald Grant Archive; **p86**: Gladskikh Tatiana/Shutterstock; **p87**: Gillespaire/Dreamstime; **p89**: The Halas and Batchelor Collection; **p90**: Elena Elisseeva/Shutterstock; **p92**: Ronald Grant Archive; **p94**: Stephen Orsillo/Shutterstock; **p95**: Photos 12/Alamy/Photolibrary; **p96**: Lebrecht Music & Arts Photo Library/Photolibrary; **p97**: Photodisc/OUP; **p99**: Corel/OUP; **p100t**: The Halas and Batchelor Collection; **p100b**: The Halas and Batchelor Collection; **p101**: Focus/Everett/Rex Features; **p107l**: Tischenko Irina/Shutterstock; **p107l**: Anthony Blake/Photolibrary; **p107r**: Benis Arapovic/Dreamstime; **p109**: OUP; **p110**: Seen/Fotolia; **p111t**: Alexandra Borsuk/Fotolia; **p111b**: Robert Byron/Dreamstime; **p112**: aopsan/ Shutterstock; **p113t**: Rex Features; **p113b**: English School/The Bridgeman Art Library/Getty Images; **p115**: Susannah Ireland/Rex Features; **p118t**: Henry Diltz/Corbis; **p118b**: Oxford Scientific/Photolibrary; **p119**: Richard Ashworth/Photolibrary; **p121**: David Hughes/Shutterstock; **p122**: Edd Westmacott./Alamy/Photolibrary; **p125**: Irinkk/ Shutterstock.

Illustrations by Flora Douville, Oxford Designers & Illustrators, Rheannon Cummins, Theresa Tibbetts, Tom Genower.

The publisher and authors are grateful for permission to reprint the following copyright material:

Alan Bennett: extracts from *The History Boys* (Faber, 2004), reprinted by permission of Faber & Faber Ltd.
Roddy Doyle: extract from *Paddy Clarke Ha Ha Ha* (Secker & Warburg, 1993), reprinted by permission of the Random House Group Ltd.
Athol Fugard: extracts from *Tsotsi* (Canongate, 2009), originally published by Ad Donker, South Africa 1980 and in Australia by The Text Publishing Co, reprinted by permission of the publishers, Canongate Books, 14 High Street, Edinburgh EH1 1TE, Text Publishing Co, and DALRO Pty Ltd, South Africa on behalf of Ad Donker.
William Golding: extracts from *Lord of the Flies* (Faber, 1954), reprinted by permission of Faber & Faber Ltd.
Seamus Heaney: 'Blackberry Picking' from *Death of a Naturalist* (Faber, 1966), reprinted by permission of Faber & Faber Ltd.
Harper Lee: extracts from *To Kill a Mockingbird* (Wm Heinemann 1960/Vintage 2004), copyright © Harper Lee, reprinted by permission of the Random House Group Ltd.
Li-Young Lee: 'Early in the Morning' from *Rose: poems* (Boa Editions, 1986), copyright © Li-Young Lee 1986, reprinted by permission of The Permissions Company, Inc on behalf of Boa Editions Ltd, www.boaeditions.org.
Edward Lucie-Smith: 'Silence' from *Changing Shape* (Carcanet, 2002), reprinted by permission of Carcanet Press Ltd.
George Orwell: extracts from *Animal Farm* (Penguin Modern Classics, 1972), copyright © George Orwell 1945, reprinted by permission of Bill Hamilton as the Literary Executor of the Estate of the late Sonia Brownell Orwell and Secker & Warburg Ltd, c/o A M Heath & Co Ltd.
J B Priestley: extract from *An Inspector Calls* (Heinemann Plays, 1992), copyright © J B Priestley 1947, 1992, reprinted by permission of United Agents on behalf of The Estate of J B Priestley.
Willy Russell: extracts from *Educating Rita* (Methuen Drama, 2007), copyright © Willy Russell 1985, reprinted by permission of Methuen Drama, an imprint of A & C Black Publishers. All rights whatsoever in this play are strictly reserved and application for performance etc must be made before rehearsal to Casarotto Ramsay & Associates Ltd, 7–12 Noel Street, London W1F 8GQ. No performance may be given unless a licence has been obtained.
Meera Syal: extracts from *Anita and Me* (Flamingo, 1997), copyright © Meera Syal 1996, reprinted by permission of HarperCollins Publishers Ltd.

Although we have made every effort to trace and contact all copyright holders before publication this has not been possible in all cases. If notified, the publisher will rectify any errors or omissions at the earliest opportunity.